Financial

Happine$$

DISCLAIMER

This book contains the opinions and ideas of its author. It is sold with the understanding that neither the author nor the publisher are engaged in rendering investment, financial, accounting, legal, tax, insurance, or other professional advice or services. If you require such advice or services, a competent professional should be consulted. The strategies outlined in this book may not be suitable for every person and are not guaranteed to produce any particular result.

No warrant is made with respect to the accuracy or completeness of the information contained herein. Both the author and publisher specifically disclaim any responsibility for any liability, loss, or risk, personal and otherwise, which is incurred as a consequence, directly or indirectly, of the use and application of any of the contents of this book.

Here is the same speech put in a way you can actually understand. This book is designed to educate you, not "sell" you. (Well, that's not quite true. I do want you to plunk down twenty dollars for the book.) No one is paying me to hype his or her products.

No individual situation is the same. One way does not work for everyone. I realize many people struggle to just survive in this world. You may find yourself in a situation where you have few options. I encourage you to find ways to apply what you read in this book as best you can. Education can help when life seems hopeless.

Find ways around the obstacles in your life. The power lies within you and your ability to change the way you think and act. Never forget that, and never give up. You truly do have the ability to change the course of your life. Believe that, and believe in yourself.

I dedicate this book to my dad, Owen Finley.

CONTENTS

Stage I: A NEW WAY OF THINKING

Stage II: **TRAVELLING FROM HERE TO THERE**

Stage III: **MISTAKES YOU MUST AVOID**

Stage IV: **LESS SPENDING EQUALS MORE SAVINGS**

Stage V: **BECOME THE WISE INVESTOR**

Stage VI: **TO GIVE IS TO LIVE**

My Story

My name is Mike Finley, and I proudly wear a pink wig wherever my travels take me. Now, before you call the police and have me committed, I would like to tell you a story, my story. I was raised in a small farm town smack-dab in the middle of the lovely state of Iowa. My upbringing was normal by most people's standards, but there were a few obstacles I had to overcome, as we all must do.

My mother died of breast cancer when I was two years old. My father dealt with this tragedy by attempting to drink his misery away. (It didn't work.) Soon he would find a lovely woman by the name of Avis, who he would marry. Avis did the best she could, but that would not last for long. Divorce and a one-parent home would take us to the end of my rather dysfunctional, but fairly typical, American childhood.

I survived high school, and a month later I was sitting at home with no clue as to what I was going to do with the rest of my life. In walked my father, who made a rather dramatic statement. He looked me straight in the eye and spoke from his heart. He said, "You are going to have to find another place to live before the year is out." *My father did not bluff.*

My dad walked away knowing what he had done. He had kick-started my life. Within a month I signed up for the United States Army, and as they say, the rest is history. I will be forever grateful to my dad for the kick in the butt I needed at that moment in my life.

One cold day in November 1982, I left my safe and secure home and the life I knew for something pretty darn scary—the United States Army. The little bird was being pushed out of the nest. It was my chance to fly. As you might imagine, it was not pretty. You see, I was entering a world where money was earned, spent, and sometimes saved by people who looked a lot like me. There was a problem. I knew nothing about money and how to manage it.

After completing my army training, I was sent to my first duty station at Fort Rucker, Alabama. This was my first real opportunity to handle money, MY MONEY! I spent plenty, saved what was left, and basically just did what most of my buddies were doing—winged it.

One day during the summer of 1985, one of my supervisors told me I should start investing in the stock market like she was doing. I said, "Sure, why not?" I had no idea what she was talking about, but what did I have to lose, right?

I was introduced to a sharp-looking professional in a suit and tie, and he told me he was there to help me achieve wealth. Within no time at all I was signing up to invest $300 a month in the stock market. Then I was ushered over to another gentlemen in the same building who looked just as impressive in his suit and tie. This life insurance expert asked me if I wanted to invest in a type of insurance policy that would grow my money. I said, "Sure, why not?" I purchased a policy called whole life. It was part insurance and part investment. Man, was I lucky. I was now an investor in stocks and insurance. I was going to be rich!

By the spring of 1986, my paycheck was getting bigger, and that meant it was time to buy a new car. That's the American way, right? Although my current vehicle was serving me well, I was impressed with my supervisor's brand new truck. He said he got a "deal" and that he could help me do the same. I said, "Sure, why not?" As I stepped onto the new-car lot, the sharp-looking salesman flew over to greet me. He peppered me with a few questions, such as how much I made and how much I could afford to fork over on a monthly basis. Before long, I was taking one of those new cars out on a test drive. Soon after, I bought it. I was a success!

The army sent me to Europe in 1989 as I continued to perform my duties as a soldier. I found a quaint place to live in downtown Schweinfurt, Germany, but it had one small problem. It was not wired to receive the one English-speaking channel (Armed Forces Network). What was I going to do? I made one of the biggest decisions of my life. I sold my television and moved in. Life would never be the same.

What does a young man do with his free time after work without a TV? I could have spent those extra hours at the local bars chasing the pretty local girls and drinking the tasty and very strong German beer, or I could have done something else. I chose to start reading books. I started reading about many topics, and before long I was finishing off two books a week. Within a few months, I had increased my interest in many topics, and one in particular, personal finance, was going to play a very big part in my future life.

One day one of my buddies stopped me and asked if I was investing in the stock market like he had heard. I stuck my chest out and said, "Yes, I do." His eyes lit up, and he asked if he could come over that evening to learn how to invest his money. I agreed to his request and made the appointment. Later that night, my friend peppered me with questions regarding the world of investing. I had no answers.

It did not take long before my chest started to deflate. I had nothing to tell my friend. As he left the apartment, I shut the door and stared at the guy in the mirror. I was twenty-five years old and still financially dumb. Could I be rich and dumb? I had a restless night of sleep as I contemplated my financial ineptitude.

The next day during lunch, I headed to the bookstore. What was I looking for? I didn't know, but I had to start somewhere, and the bookstore seemed a reasonable place to begin this journey. Lo and behold, I found a book titled, *Wealth Without Risk*, by Charles Givens. I picked it up, thumbed through a few pages, said what the hell, and paid the lady at the counter twenty dollars for the book.

I took that book home and read it. Actually, I did more skimming than reading, because most of the information was flying right over my financially illiterate head. Nonetheless, I did learn a few things, and one point stuck out above all others. This one point changed me and the course of my life. Charles Givens taught me:

I am the answer.

After finishing my first book on money, I picked up another and then another. Slowly but surely, I started to understand what had previously been unknown to me. I was becoming financially literate, one book and one author at a time. This process continued over the next six months.

After those many months of self-education, it was time to start taking action. I started with my very first net-worth statement. I was excited. I was finally going to find out just how rich I was.

I had to identify where I currently was financially. I took my assets (real estate, cars, cash, stocks, bonds, etc.) and subtracted my liabilities (debt from my car loan, home loan, credit cards, student loans, etc.). It took some work, but my net-worth statement was done. What did I learn? I was worth a negative two-thousand and some-odd dollars. *I was broke.* I was stunned by this reality. Instead of being rich, I was poor. This highlighted something very important to me. Financial illiteracy got me to this point, and if I was ever going to get out of this situation, I had to change. I did.

My next stop was the investment broker. I walked in to his office in downtown Schweinfurt and politely told him to redeem my shares in the high-commission and high-fee mutual fund that I owned. (I finally understood my investments.)

The well-dressed and smooth-talking broker tried to "talk me off the ledge." What he did not know was that I was now empowered by my newfound financial knowledge. I was firm, and I was clear. Sell my investments, and close the account. My next stop was the life insurance expert. I called him up in the States and cancelled the unnecessary and expensive whole-life policy. *My life was changing.*

Next up, the debt. I reviewed my car-purchase contract. I was paying over 13 percent on a five-year loan that included an extended warranty. Dumb, dumb, and dumb. I stopped everything I was doing and put all of my money toward paying off the debt. I sacrificed immediate gratification for long-term benefits. I wanted a better life.

Next, I looked at my credit cards and saw nothing but red. I was paying 20 percent on "stuff" that long ago had left my life. I designed a plan to pay off the credit cards, and then I did it. I was taking control of my life.

I continued to further my financial education as the years went on, and I kept doing what was right for my particular situation. This meant developing habits I could sustain. I still stumbled at times. I fell victim to advertising, savvy salespeople, and the occasional dumb investment, but I kept learning. I had to learn to just say NO to all those "smart" people in the pretty outfits with all the initials after their names.

Let's fast-forward to the age of forty-five. Every year since I was twenty-five, I had been identifying my financial progress by tracking my net worth, instead of my income or my "stuff." As you may recall, I was worth nothing when I was twenty-five. When I reached forty-five, I was worth more than a million dollars!

I had reached financial freedom, but that is not the end of the story. There is more to life than money, and that is one of the overriding themes you will see throughout this book.

What about the pink wig? Don't worry, we will get to that later in the book. Just stay with me as we head out on a journey of self-discovery, finding answers to some very important questions.

Be daring, be different, be impractical, be anything that will assert integrity of purpose and imaginative vision against the play-it-safers, the creatures of the commonplace, the slaves of the ordinary.

- **Cecil Beaton**

Foreword

Throughout history, many of our most brilliant entrepreneurs, artists, architects, and scientists were initially seen by many to be "crazy." It seems almost inevitable that those who bring forth ideas challenging the conventional wisdom are considered out of touch with reality. Unlike most of us, Mike Finley does not shy away from being unconventional.

Mike embraces the expectation that his ideas about the connection between financial literacy and real happiness will be criticized by some as crazy. In other words, he willfully stands with others who defy the conventional wisdom in order to make our world better. Hence, the pink wig symbolizing his insistence on not conforming to the widely accepted ideas about spending, saving, and investing.

The title of this book invites readers to take a journey that the financial industry, advertising corporations, investment brokers, insurance companies, and others who thrive on financial ignorance do not want us to take.

Mike invites us to be crazy enough to learn that we can manage our finances in ways that contribute to our prosperity and happiness, without relying on so-called experts who frequently make us poorer rather than richer. I do not know anyone who is more qualified to guide us on this journey than the "Crazy" Man in the Pink Wig.

Like most of us, Mike entered into adulthood without much knowledge about how to make good choices about spending, saving, and investing. Unlike most of us, he quickly learned two things about his lack of financial literacy. First, that it could send him straight to the poor house. Second, that he had the power to become as knowledgeable about money management as any of the so-called money management experts. Armed with these insights, he embarked on several years of a comprehensive study into every aspect of personal finance.

Nothing connected to individual and family finances escaped Mike's thorough analysis. By the time he reached the zenith of his research, Mike Finley, a first sergeant in the United States Army, had used his newfound knowledge to become a millionaire. At the age of forty-five, he retired from the army comfortable in the knowledge that he would never again have to work for anyone except himself.

Educating others about the path to happiness through achieving financial literacy is the work Mike does today. No one does it better.

Over the years, I've watched the "Crazy" Man in the Pink Wig teach university students and faculty from all walks of life how to find new kinds of freedom and happiness as they learn how to more intelligently spend, save, and invest their money. One of the most amazing parts of being an observer to this process is watching the changes in the lives of Mike's students as their fear and anxiety about money is replaced by knowledge, power, and happiness.

Your path to financial literacy, and the happiness it can bring, will not necessarily be easy. Along the way, it will be important to remind yourself that happiness and fulfillment will be found in the journey as much as in the destination. But rest assured that with this book, the road forward will be made clear by someone who started with next to nothing and then created for himself both great wealth and great happiness.

Work hard to incorporate what you learn from this book into your daily life. Believe in yourself, and believe in the "Crazy" Man in the Pink Wig. A future of financial well-being and happiness awaits you.

Sincerely,
Joe Gorton, Ph. D.
University of Northern Iowa

Testimonials

"The knowledge and resources that Michael has provided me have truly changed my life. I am lucky to have begun my journey to becoming financial literate early in life..."—**Dustin,** Student, Age 21

"Becoming financially literate has been one of the most gratifying choices I've ever made. It's an amazing moment when you realize how simple it is to take a step back from our hyper-consumerist culture and gain control of your finances, mindset, and your life...." —**Nate**, Collegiate Staff with The Navigators, Age 21

"I've learned that financial happiness is a life-long process that we must work on every day. A crazy man in a pink wig helped me by teaching me to learn the vocabulary and importance of saving my money...."—**Jon**, CNC Machinist, Age 22

"Mike's plan is the most logical self-improvement plan I have encountered. Mike takes the gimmicks and fancy language out of personal finance and explains how easily YOU can be the answer to your financial life...." — **Aaron**, Teacher, Age 25

"I truly believe that knowing personal finance is vital to having a more relaxed life. Financial literacy has changed my life and brought me happiness...." —**Azam**, MBA Student, Age 29

"The financial service industry is a marketing machine out to convince the average consumer that bloated expensive products are best. Mike is arming the consumer with their best weapon—financial literacy." —**Tracy**, Former Financial Advisor and Insurance Agent, Age 30

"...Now I have the knowledge, tools, and confidence to make the right choices for myself and am working to improve my financial future every day...." —**Molly**, Iowa Air National Guard and College Student, Age 30

"Because of Mike's advice, my wife and I will be able to retire at the age of sixty! His advice also allowed us to put four kids through college and begin a college savings account for our grandchildren...."—**Patrick,** LTC, USAR, Director of Human Resources Operations & Veteran Initiatives, MedSynergies, Inc., Age 49

"Mike gave me the tools to help me see I was headed toward a financial disaster if I didn't change my way of thinking...." — **Kim,** Respiratory Therapist, Age 50

"... *Financial Happine$$* stood out by presenting the most in-depth and research-based information in simple, understandable language. *Financial Happine$$* teaches you how to develop a wealth-building mindset that's not based on greed and materialism. I highly recommend this book." —**Holly,** Medical Researcher, Age 50

"In today's modern world of massive advertising, huge consumer debt, and rampant materialism, Mike Finley provided the sane voice that a person is not insane to save, spend smartly, and invest for a life filled with happiness and success. Mike reinforced the values that my Depression Era parents instilled in me every day of my childhood, and his notes have helped me share these values effectively with my own children..." —**Pete,** Inventor, Engineer, Age 55

"Mike has made a significant impression on me about financial literacy, but while doing so he has also shown me how to keep it in perspective while finding happiness in life." —**Larry,** Retired, Age 63

"Mike showed me how to reallocate my thoughts about how to handle my financial situation. It has been a lifesaver for me to have the peace of mind that is following." —**Linda,** College Professor, Age 69

"Michael gave me the confidence to take responsibility for my financial happiness after being with a financial adviser for a number of years. His excellent advice helped me overcome the fear of failure. You CAN teach an old dog new tricks." —**Beverly,** Homemaker, Age 76

Introduction

I have observed over the years that many people who strive to become educated on money go to the wrong places to receive that education (just like I did). Going to a financial advisor to learn about investing is a bad idea. Going to a life insurance agent to become knowledgeable about life insurance is a really bad idea. Going to a car salesman to learn about the best car deals is ridiculous. Hold it, you knew that last point, didn't you? Those three salespeople belong in the same category because of the conflict of interest they bring with them. Do not allow yourself to be educated by anyone who makes their living based on commissions. You need to go elsewhere for your financial education.

So why should you listen to me? That is a good question, and I do want you to stay very skeptical when ANYONE is trying to help you with your money.

Here are two key reasons why I ask you to trust me. First, I have no conflict of interest. I teach; I don't sell. (Nobody pays me a dime). The second key point is my trump card. I have learned from the best teachers.

Jane Bryant Quinn, Jonathon Clements, and Eric Tyson taught me about personal finance and how to manage each dollar wisely.

Dave Ramsey and Michael Mihalik taught me about the evils of debt and how to eliminate it from my life.

William Bernstein, Burton Malkiel, Daniel Solin and Warren Buffett taught me how to invest my money by becoming knowledgeable about modern portfolio theory, the history of the markets, the psychological state of human beings, and the businesspeople who are trying to take their cut.

Thomas Stanley and Keith Cameron Smith taught me who the real millionaires are, how they think, and how they act. They also taught me what the fakes look like.

Vicki Robin, Joe Dominguez, and Tim Kasser taught me how to see the real value of money and how materialism could rob me of a better and happier life.

Jason Zweig taught me that emotions play a big part in the decisions I make, and if I were ever going to take control of my money, I had to take control of my feelings.

John Bogle built the foundation, the Vanguard Group (an investment management company owned by its investors), which has helped thousands of people just like you and me achieve their financial dreams at minimal cost. Mr. Bogle taught me the value of passively invested no-load index funds, where to find them, and how to invest in them.

Finally, I owe Charles Givens the most thanks. He taught me that I am the answer to my financial future. He was right.

This book is for people who don't read many books and may not make a lot of money. As for the rest of you who do read often and may make a nice income, don't worry; you might just want to give this book a chance. Knowledge can come from the unlikeliest of places.

This book is my way of sharing what I have learned. Some things I learned the smart way, by educating myself before taking action, and some things I learned the hard way. I took action before the appropriate knowledge was acquired.

I encourage you to read this book from start to finish. I will start you in one place and drop you off in another. It will be a journey with a few real world examples sprinkled in gray. KEY POINT: This is not a "how to get rich" book. This book is designed to help you:

Achieve financial freedom and find true happiness.

I have travelled this journey. I know where many of the craters are located that you must avoid. I also know how to refocus your efforts as you stay on this challenging and rewarding path.

You will see some overlap in a few of the lessons. This should not surprise you. Much of personal finance overlaps into different parts of our daily lives. When you see information discussed more than once, you can bet it's important. This journey requires a different way of speaking, thinking and acting. Stay open to its message.

How much you learn will have a lot to do with how open you are to changing the way you think, which will ultimately lead to what you actually do. I simply ask you to keep an open mind and trust me as you would any other person who wears a pink wig (wink, wink).

This manual is all about helping improve not only your financial life, but also the rest of your life. This book deals with much more than simple personal finance. That part is less complicated than you are led to believe. The psychological part is not so easy.

Financial happine$$ is a journey that will take time. I believe in your ability to change your financial future, but it won't be easy. I am here to assist you, but I need your help. Together we can do this. Before we get underway, I have a story to share that should help get us started.

I call this the Snickers problem. Once upon a time, a mother needed groceries to feed her family of three (Mom, Dad, and precocious little Johnny). Mom went to the local grocery store with Johnny in tow as she searched for a family meal for that evening. As the two of them walked the aisles, Johnny saw a big and delicious Snickers candy bar.

Johnny abruptly stopped what he was doing and told his mother he wanted that Snickers. Johnny's mother shook her head from side to side as she stated, "That would only spoil your dinner." Johnny did not like that answer. As his mother attempted to pull Johnny along, Johnny dug his heels in and made his stance very clear.

Johnny wanted the Snickers, and he wanted it *now*! As expected, Johnny's mother became quite upset and emphatically told Johnny no. At this point, all hell broke loose. Johnny threw himself on the floor and started screaming and hollering at the top of his lungs.

As the other store patrons looked on with great disdain, Johnny's mother just stood there, horrified at what she was seeing. She quickly picked Johnny up by the collar and dragged his screaming little body out of the store. They left without the dinner fixings and without the Snickers.

What is the problem here? Is it the Snickers? Did a candy bar cause this mess? I think you know the answer, and I think most people know the answer. Johnny is a spoiled brat. That is the problem.

If Johnny's mother ever wants to fix the Snickers problem, she first must fix the brat problem. Simply eliminating Snickers from the shelves of the store will not do it. Soon there will be a Kit Kat problem. What if those are taken away? The Cheetos problem begins. I think you get my point. Fixing the brat problem makes the other problems go away without ever having to directly deal with them. Financial literacy followed by action will cause many problems in your life to go away.

This story takes us to the core message of this book. Millions of people spend their days trying to fix Snickers problems. They use credit to buy "stuff" that will make them popular/beautiful/successful/happy. They chase after more and more money to make life "better." They put a great deal of trust in the financial-industry "experts" as they seek great riches from their "amazing" talents. Yet many people never really get down to the core issue that will help them reach a sustained level of joy and inner peace in their lives. Stay with me as we explore this topic in more depth in the following pages. Let's get started.

The one who follows the crowd will usually get no further than the crowd. The one who walks alone, is likely to find himself in places no one has ever been.

- **Albert Einstein**

Stage I

A NEW WAY OF THINKING

1

THE FINANCIAL LITERACY JOURNEY

The financial literacy journey that ultimately leads to a higher level of inner peace and personal happiness can be achieved, but not without some true insight, sacrifice, and hard work. Let's take a look at what it will involve, as you prepare for this challenging and rewarding journey.

- *I am.* I am the answer to my financial future. It's up to me. I must take control of my life.

- *Knowledge.* I must educate myself *before* making financial decisions. This will involve a commitment to education outside the classroom with teachers, not salespeople. This is my responsibility.

- *ACTION.* I must take action with what I learn. Being financially smart and doing nothing with the information will accomplish nothing. I must act!

- *Keep Doing.* I must keep doing what is right financially one week, one month, one year, and one decade at a time. I will stick with it through good times and bad.

- *Just say NO!* Just say no to materialism (defining myself by the stuff I own) and the crocodiles (salespeople who feed off my financial ignorance).

- *Patience.* Time is on my side. I will be patient as my financial plan unfolds over long periods of time. I will get rich slowly through the amazing thing called compound interest.

- *Financial Freedom.* Financial freedom can be achieved if I am willing to commit to the process of learning and executing my financial plan. Saving = Freedom = Opportunities.

- *Live MY Dreams.* I will live the life of my dreams and not someone else's. Financial freedom will provide me the opportunity to do just that as I reach for something greater.

- *Give.* I will learn to give. I will give a positive attitude. I will give of my experience. I will give of my expertise. I will give of my time. I will give of my possessions. And yes, I will give of my money. Giving will help create a world I want to live in.

- *Happiness.* Happiness comes to those who follow their dreams and share what they know with others. I want to be happy, and there is a path to get me there. I believe it, and I believe in myself. I realize there will be difficulties along the way, and I am willing to make the necessary sacrifices as I reach for something greater.

Just as treasures are uncovered from the earth, so virtue appears from good deeds, and wisdom appears from a pure and peaceful mind. To walk safely through the maze of human life, one needs the light of wisdom and the guidance of virtue.

- The Buddha

2

THE START

What ran through your mind when you read my story? Was I an idiot for being financially illiterate at the age of twenty-five? Did you feel sorry for me, or did you feel a sense of empathy for my plight? Did you shake your head at my behavior, or did you acknowledge that you have also made some of the same boneheaded mistakes?

KEY POINT: The past is the past. I screwed up, and I have learned from my mistakes. I will avoid repeating them in the future. It's important not to beat yourself up about mistakes you have made in your past. We all have regrets, and we have all made mistakes. Let them go, and move forward along this journey.

There comes a time in our lives when we must start anew. I tell my story to make a clear and profound point. My false start was the beginning of a financially literate life that gradually led to financial freedom and, ultimately, to true happiness. Let's take a look at what options I had available to me at the beginning of this journey.

I could have chosen *option #1*. I could have played down my financially illiteracy and simply brushed off my friend's questions as meaningless. This option would have eventually taken me down the path of financial impoverishment until one day my bills would overwhelm my income. I would be living paycheck to paycheck (best-case scenario) just hoping to pay my bills each and every month. Lucky for me, I passed on this option.

I might have chosen *option #2*. I could have gone to a "better" financial expert and had him or her teach me how to invest my money in a "better" way. Many people choose this path. They rely on others to do their financial thinking for them. In some ways, I had been following this path, which served me poorly to say the least. I passed on this option.

I chose *option #3*. I chose to become self-educated. I chose to become my own financial expert, which meant I had to find independent financial teachers to guide me. I did this through books written by authors who did not have a conflict of interest in the information they were sharing. They were teachers.

Did I become financially literate overnight? Nope. I educated myself over long stretches of time. This was a process, which led me on a journey toward becoming financially literate. There were ups and downs as the learning curve did its thing, but gradually I changed my ways, and in so doing, I changed the course of my life.

What catalyst will start you down your journey? How will you find the motivation that will ultimately take you in a different and better direction financially?

Time does not stop for anyone. In a blink of an eye you will find yourself fifty, sixty, maybe seventy years old. When you look back on your life, what will you see? There is no better time to start your journey toward financial happine$$ than right now. Begin today!

You build on failure. You use it as a stepping stone. Close the door on the past. You don't try to forget the mistakes, but you don't dwell on it. You don't let it have any of your energy, or any of your time, or any of your space.

- **Johnny Cash**

3

DO YOU CUT THE
ENDS OFF?

How many of your daily money decisions have something to do with the way you were raised? For many of us, the answer is a lot. Many times we make day-to-day money choices using our hearts rather than our heads. Or maybe we are just repeating what we saw or heard many years ago. Are you cutting the ends off your ham?

I have a story I would like to share with you. Once upon a time, a curious young girl by the name of Martha asked her mother why she cut off both ends of the ham before she put it in the pan and then into the oven. Her mother said, "That's the way I've always done it. That's the way my mother did it."

Martha was puzzled and confused by what she heard, so she decided to pay a visit to her grandmother where she posed the same question. Martha's grandmother paused, and then said, "That's the way I've always done it. That's the way my mother did it."

Still not satisfied, Martha went to the nursing home where she could ask the same question of her great grandmother. Why did she cut off the ends of the ham before putting it into the oven? This very old woman looked at sweet little Martha and said, "The pan was too small, honey; I had to cut off the ends so the ham would fit." 1

Why do people cut off the ends without knowing why? We mimic the older people in our life. We attempt to emulate the adults, the ones who seemed to know what they were doing.

We secretly want to be like those role models that hovered over us as young people. We may fight it as young adults, we may even scream our contempt as teenagers, but the reality is the acorn does not fall far from the tree. Or does it?

It is critical that you step back and really take stock of how you feel about money. *Ask why.* This requires quite a bit of self-reflection as you become aware of who you are and why you do what you do with the money that comes in and leaves your life.

I encourage you to sit down with your loved ones and talk about money matters. How did your parents deal with money? Were your parents spenders or savers? What drove their money habits way back when, and what drives yours today?

Take this opportunity to look back, review what you think you know, and take the time to understand how you got here. Now is the time to evaluate why you do what you do with your money. It may just be time to stop cutting the ends off that ham.

I believe that one defines oneself by reinvention. To not be like your parents. To not be like your friends. To be yourself. To cut yourself out of stone.

- **Henry Rollins**

4

THE ELEPHANT

Are you familiar with how a young circus elephant is trained? Good news, I have completed my research on this very intriguing matter, and I want to share all that I know.

When a baby elephant is quite young and not so powerful, his trainer will tie him to a steel pole with nothing more than a simple rope. This rope is strong enough to stop this young squirt from getting away, and while the elephant struggles to tear himself loose, he comes up empty, because he just does not have the strength to free himself at this stage in his young life. After a while, the young elephant comes to his senses and just quits trying. He realizes he can't get loose, and so he just settles into his predicament. 2 Isn't that fascinating? No? Okay, there is more to the story, so please be patient with me.

As you know, young elephants gradually become big elephants. I mean *really* big elephants. They become so big and so mighty that they could do some major damage to anyone or anything that stands in their path. Here is where it gets interesting.

The elephant trainer never stops tying the elephant to that small pole with the same rope that held it as a little elephant. Yep, that little rope with the little pole is still holding that BIG elephant. Could he snap that rope in two? Oh, yeah. Could he probably pull that small pole out of the ground? Perhaps. And yet, neither of these things will happen. Why? It would be futile in his mind. He never could and never will. That's just the way it is, and that's the way it will always be. That's life as he knows it.

We learn plenty as young people. We learn by what we see. We learn by what the giants tell us (adults who also go by the name of trainer). And I think it's pretty clear that we also learn based on how we feel. There is nothing too insightful there, right? Well, what about all that crap we learned that wasn't true. You know, stuff like you're stupid, you're weird, you're ugly, you're strange, you're weak, and maybe someone even said you were worthless. Does that sound familiar to anyone?

Are you still tied to that pole with that old piece of rope? You do realize that you can snap that rope at any time, right? When you are truly ready to change, you will change.

You should challenge what you know when you are presented with new information that conflicts with what you have learned in the past. You can be the person you want to be instead of what someone else wanted you to be. You are the answer. Go ahead; say it few times in the mirror to make sure it sinks in. Your financial future depends on YOU. Believe it.

You control your attitude, your thoughts, and much of what you do, and I am here to remind you of that very simple point. It might just be time to snap that rope and move on to a different life, a better life, and ultimately a happier life.

It takes courage to be a real winner, not a winner in the sense of beating out someone else by always insisting on coming out on top, but a winner at responding to life. It takes courage to experience the freedom that comes with autonomy, courage to take a stand in an unpopular cause, courage to choose authenticity over approval and to choose it again and again, courage to accept the responsibility for your own choice, and indeed, courage to be the unique person you really are.

- **Muriel James and Dorothy Jongeward**, *Born to Win*

Don't Believe Everything You Hear

The comments below look rather foolish today. Just because someone says it, does not mean it is so. Believe in YOU.

He was told he lacked imagination. Walt Disney disagreed, and millions of children are thankful he did.

He was told he was stupid. Thomas Edison kept trying.

He was fired from Universal Studios. They told him his Adam's apple was too big. Clint Eastwood pushed the negative words aside.

He was told to go back to driving a truck. Elvis Presley chose to sing.

He was rejected thirty times with his first book. Steven King tried thirty-one times.

They were told their sound wasn't good, and guitar music was on the way out. The Beatles kept playing.

He was thought to be mentally handicapped, slow, and antisocial. He did not speak until he was four. Albert Einstein stayed with it.

She was fired for being unfit for TV. Oprah Winfrey kept going.

Every single studio in Hollywood turned down George Lucas and his film, *Star Wars*. He made it himself. The rest is history.

He was called a hippie and odd. He got fired from his own company, so he started a new one. Steve Jobs changed the world.

5

KINDERGARTEN

How far in life do you think you and I would have gotten if we had stopped in kindergarten? I think we can both agree that it would look pretty darn ugly. Luckily, all of us passed that difficult time of learning the alphabet and playing well with others, and we headed off to first grade with our heads held high, proud of what we had done. There is another type of kindergarten; it's called financial kindergarten. It's a pretty inviting place, but the room is crowded.

What is financial kindergarten? I see it as no different from the academic world of kindergarten. We all know how that goes. We start to learn a few basic principles, such as the alphabet, how to color inside the lines, that hitting other kids gets us into trouble. Once we get those difficult things down, they shove us off to the next grade with a bit of fanfare and plenty of pats on our heads. Onward and upward, young soul!

In financial kindergarten, we also must learn a few basic principles before proceeding forward to the next grade. We must learn how and where to save our money, how to manage credit and limit debt, how to distinguish between a need and a want, and what kind of insurance we need and what type we should avoid.

It is also important to learn what a good investment is and what a bad investment looks like (there are many). These are the basics, and they must be learned if financial literacy is going to play an important part in our lives. Without these basics, financial happine$$ will be very difficult to attain in your lifetime.

Here is a question: What happens to little Johnny in the academic world if he has difficulty coloring inside the lines? He receives a pat on the head and first grade, here he comes! In financial kindergarten, there is no passing until you are proficient at everything you need to know. No pat on the head, no lollipop, and no first grade. As a matter of fact, you can easily find yourself missing recess because your kindergarten teacher has locked the doors and left you with no key.

We *all* start in financial kindergarten. Some just never graduate. Yes, they are stuck in financial kindergarten with no way of getting out. They don't have the key. You need that key to get you out of kindergarten and into first grade. Many years back, I found the key that helped me escape financial kindergarten. Find the right teachers who will educate you on money matters, while avoiding the salespeople who will sell you on products that make THEM rich.

Where does a person start? *Personal Finance for Dummies* by Eric Tyson is a good place to begin. This book is suited for people who are still in financial kindergarten. I don't expect you to learn algebra, *The Four Pillars of Investing*, by William Bernstein, in kindergarten. That will come later as you gain a deeper knowledge about this world of money and how to effectively grow it over long periods of time.

We must progress one financial grade at a time as we learn and apply our newfound financial knowledge. KEY POINT: You are allowed to progress at your own pace. You can go from kindergarten to the fifth grade in one year. Start!

Education is not the filling of a pail, but the lighting of a fire.

- **William Butler Yeats**

6

ARE YOU AN OSTRICH?

So what is an ostrich, exactly? It is an animal that will stick its head in the sand with the other ostriches when life gets tough. (Yes, I realize an ostrich lays its head on the sand rather than sticking it in the sand, but the metaphor works here, so cut me some slack, okay?)

Why do humans take on some of the habits of an ostrich? Life is hard, and many times it is easier to stick your head in the sand. I get that, but it doesn't mean you should do it. Let's take a look at a few behaviors and attitudes that will not serve you well in life.

- *Fear:* I'm afraid I will screw things up. I think I'll hide.

- *Ignorance:* I don't know what to do, so I'll stay clueless.

- *Bravado:* I know what I am doing. Leave me alone.

- *Follow the Crowd:* I will do what everyone else does. It's safe.

- *Apathy:* It looks like too much work, and it's boring anyway.

- *I am poor:* None of this stuff applies to me. I'm broke.

- *I don't have time:* Life is hectic, maybe another day.

Do any one of these statements relate to you? Is it possible more than one sounds familiar? Whatever your reason for being an ostrich, there are a few things that you need to know if you choose that path. Bankruptcy courts are full of ostriches. Debt collection agencies have ostriches on speed dial!

Ostriches are much more prone to having problems with anxiety and emotional instability as they live a life avoiding the hard and difficult decisions. They end up succumbing to fear, and they allow this deadly disease to defeat them. *Do what is difficult, and life will be easy. Do what is easy, and life will be difficult.*

I have never met anyone who said they were an ostrich, but I can identify them very quickly by what they say and, more importantly, what they do regarding their personal finances. Believe me, it is not that hard. They stick out just like that big gangly bird does. You must avoid becoming an ostrich if you desire a more financially free life. If you currently are an ostrich, it is time to change your ways.

How? You take baby steps (start reading *Personal Finance for Dummies*). This is not that complicated. Every journey starts with the first step. You have got to take that first step, and there is no better time than right now.

It's time to start pulling your head out of the sand. Don't beat yourself up about it—we have all played the part of the Ostrich at different stages in our life—just do it. Besides, who wants to be an ostrich?

I learned that courage was not the absence of fear, but the triumph over it. The brave man is not he who does not feel afraid, but he who conquers that fear.

- **Nelson Mandela**

7

TO BE, OR NOT TO BE

Why is it necessary to learn about this boring financial stuff? Isn't it easier to just pay someone to handle these complicated matters? Why does it really matter whether you understand how credit cards work? Why you should avoid buying or leasing a new car? How do you invest your money without paying commissions? And what type of life insurance, if any, is right for you?

Why is not the question you should be asking. *Why not*, should be. Why not you? Why can't you live a financially free life that involves enough money and the fun and freedom that brings meaning to your life without incurring debt and the stress attached to it?

The short answer is *you can*, but it requires a strong will, a bit of stubbornness, and a willingness to learn and apply what is right for you. It takes a financially literate person who follows up their education with very specific actions that develop over time into repeatable habits.

Financial literacy does not care what color you are. It doesn't care what religion you follow. It doesn't care what political party you affiliate with. It doesn't care if you are old or young, pretty or plain, big or small. Financial literacy doesn't care if you have multiple college degrees, or if you barely made it through high school (that would be me).

Financial literacy becomes that equal opportunity employer that can help anyone who is willing to help himself or herself. It's time for you to help yourself move in a more positive financial direction. Make the commitment today through language, thought and action.

William Shakespeare posed a very serious question once upon a time. His point was death; my point is financial literacy. To be or not to be financially literate is the question I want you to ask yourself not just today, but for many days and years to come.

You can change your financial life, and the financial lives around you. The life that you lead will have an impact on the people who you come into contact with, and that certainly includes your family, your friends, and even the strangers that find their way into your life.

YOU change the environment.

Financial literacy requires your willingness to learn, change, and grow. It also requires action once you learn what needs to be done. You must be a doer in life if you want to live out your dreams and aspirations. Believe in yourself and your abilities. There really is no other option worth considering. Choose financial happine$$.

It is not the critic who counts; not the man who points out how the strong man stumbles, or where the doer of deeds could have done them better. The credit belongs to the man who is actually in the arena, whose face is marred by dust and sweat and blood; who strives valiantly; who errs, who comes short again and again, because there is no effort without error and shortcoming; but who does actually strive to do the deeds; who knows great enthusiasms, the great devotions; who spends himself in a worthy cause; who at the best knows in the end the triumph of high achievement, and who at the worst, if he fails, at least fails while daring greatly, so that his place shall never be with those cold and timid souls who neither know victory nor defeat.

- **Theodore Roosevelt**

8

THE PROCESS OF ACCRETION

How many of you are familiar with the term *accretion*? Maybe you have learned about this process gradually over time. (That was a joke by the way.) This concept goes something like this. The process of accretion involves growth by gradual addition over time as one concept builds off a previous concept.

We humans learn using a cumulative approach in which one concept starts to build off a previous concept, which had been built from a previous concept. This is an important point in understanding financial literacy and the future that will be yours. I think of it as layering what you learn, one concept on top of another.

When a person begins to learn about money, it is new and usually foreign to them. This applies to everyone. Here is where people like Burton Malkiel, William Bernstein, Jane Bryant Quinn, Eric Tyson, John Bogle and Warren Buffett separate themselves from the pack. They build on that initial education one layer at a time.

Think of the process of building a house. The first time a builder attempts it, there will certainly be much to learn. Gradually, the builder will understand how to build a better home as their knowledge builds. Each layer of knowledge is built off the previous layer. This explains the process of accretion. So you might be asking, "How does this apply to me and this idea of financial happine$$?"

Building upon our financial literacy enables us to acquire and understand new information as we layer our education. Gradually, the process of accretion helps us accumulate more and more financial knowledge. At some point, the fire is lit as we start "connecting the dots" within the world of personal finance.

We start to piece information together into a more cohesive and logical way that makes this world of money more understandable. We can start to develop a new way of thinking as we develop new habits that take us down a path that we can follow as our accumulated information builds and builds and builds.

The lessons that follow will give you a simple approach to financial literacy that should cause you to think about the subject differently and ask more questions, which in turn leads you to educate yourself further from other sources, which in turn causes you to ask even more questions.

These new sources of information will eventually lead you to even more sources of new information. Imagine a snowball rolling down a mountain. Little by little, it accumulates more and more snow (financial knowledge). Soon, it will be unstoppable as momentum takes hold. This can be you. This should be you. Make this you.

Allow yourself to hear your own still small voice; to believe in your truth; to find a place within of safety and peace; and to understand the depth and truth of your own feelings. Life is meant to be lived—not endured or existing feeling totally stressed out. You have the power to create a life in which you are respected for who you are—valued, cherished, and celebrated! Life is too short to allow other people to steal your joy. You have something special...you have GREATNESS within you!

- **Les Brown**

9

A BETTER DAY IS COMING

I doubt that many of us have gone a day without hearing about how bad life is. How you have no shot at achieving whatever it is your parents or grandparents achieved. You are screwed, and there is very little you can do about it. Are those messages right?

It makes good copy for the folks in the media business to print and spout off all the bad news they can find. If they can't find it, they create it! They feed off the emotions of their followers. My recommendation is to start tuning them out. Just because the media states something is news does not make it so. Push the negative news and the negative people who spew it out of your life. Those negative voices will not serve you well today or going forward with your future life.

No one has ever lived in a more amazing time. Do you realize that you have more access to information than Albert Einstein or Thomas Edison ever did? I wonder what those amazing men would say today if someone showed them how to Google a topic of interest using this thing called a computer? I am sure they would be astonished as they explored worlds previously unknown to them.

So why am I attempting to keep your hope alive in the face of all the negative news and commentary? You need hope if you ever want to move beyond the spot you are standing in.

You need hope to be willing to learn and take a chance and grow, whether that means starting a business, saving and investing in the stock market, or maybe buying your first home. You need hope to reach for something greater.

Push aside the naysayers in this world, and move forward toward your goals and aspirations. Tune out that negative chatter that enters your head as well. Negativity causes you to do nothing, as you fear what could happen if you did something. This has been called stinkin' thinkin' by some. Steer clear of negative people and their defeatist attitudes. It can seep into you and will not help your financial future.

It will take a great deal of fortitude and probably a bit of stubbornness to overcome all those folks who tell you that it cannot be done. It can be done, and you can do it. It takes hope and a belief in your abilities to change the course of your life.

Find the people in your world who will encourage and support your dreams. Identify these individuals, and don't let go. They will help you find what you are seeking. What if there is no one physically around you that fits that bill? Go to the library. Go to the bookstore. Google it!

There are some amazing people waiting to provide the wisdom and knowledge you will need as your life unfolds. Find them, and learn from those remarkable people.

You may find this chapter hard to directly link to financial happine$$. Yet, I hope you can see how the negative rhetoric all around you can stop you from ever changing your financial life and achieving your dreams. This is a battle for your life and what it will look like. You must win this battle. The future will be full of amazing people. Be one of them.

Everyone has been made for some particular work, and the desire for that work has been put in every heart.

- **Rumi**

10

THE INTELLIGENT QUOTIENT

Do you need a master's degree in finance to achieve wealth? Nope. As a matter of fact, it could be detrimental to your financial future. What? Overly confident people with multiple degrees can, and many times do, hurt themselves by overanalyzing their financial life and trying to outsmart people who are trying to outsmart them.

Financial literacy does not require a degree in finance or business or any degree for that matter. I would even take this one step further by saying that those degrees have very little to do with achieving financial freedom. There are other elements that are much more important for building wealth, such as self-discipline, courage, strength of character, imagination, focus, consistency, introspection, willingness to change when presented new information, persistence, and don't forget that thing they call self-sufficiency.

So you might be thinking that I am attacking a formal academic education. I am not. That education (any degree) will most likely provide you a broad perspective of life with the opportunity to make more money during your lifetime (diplomas open up doors). What a formal academic education does not do is make you financially literate.

There is a stark difference between performing well in school and having a high financial IQ (high level of financial education). These are not one in the same, and it is very important to understand this key point as you move along in your life. Let's take a look at one pretty clear example of two people and how their lives could end up.

Cynthia is a physicist with a PhD who makes $200,000 per year. Bob is a beginning plumber with a high school diploma who makes $50,000 per year. Who do you think will do better financially in life? Our initial thought would be Cynthia, right? Not so fast.

Just because Cynthia has multiple degrees and makes a great deal of money does not mean she knows anything about money and how to manage it. It does mean she knows a lot about the theory of relativity and the nature of black holes in deep space. Cynthia could be one very educated and well-paid financial dummy.

Bob is quite capable of taking his yearly salary of $50,000 and growing it to a point where he will be financially free one day. This means his income from his investments will be enough to cover his living expenses. He will not have to work (he may choose to work, but he does not have to). This has nothing to do with Bob being the smartest person in the room, but rather it has everything to do with Bob acquiring a high degree of financial knowledge and taking action with what he has learned.

If Cynthia does not acquire a financial education, she is most likely destined to live paycheck to paycheck no matter how big her salary becomes over the years. It is not how much money you make; it is how much money you end up keeping that counts. Never forget that very important point.

Often we are caught in a mental trap of seeing enormously successful people and thinking they are where they are because they have some special gift. Yet a closer look shows that the greatest gift that extraordinarily successful people have over the average person is their ability to get themselves to take action.

- **Anthony Robbins**

Actual Wealth vs. Looking the Part

Bob		Cynthia
$50,000	Yearly Income	$200,000
20%	Savings Rate	0%
$10,000	Yearly Savings	$0
9%	Investment Return After Costs	0%
$193,744	10 Years Later	$0
$644,168	20 Years Later	$0
$1,748,317	30 Years Later	$0

You can appear to be rich by spending all of your money on stuff (you are what you have), or you can actually become rich over time by saving your money consistently and automatically (pay yourself first) while investing efficiently at the lowest possible cost (no-load index mutual funds). The example shows a simple interest calculation in the first year and the compounding effect that takes place one decade at a time. The choice is yours.

11

WILL YOU ACCEPT IT OR REJECT IT?

You were born into a society without your permission or your request. My question to you is: Will you accept it or reject it? What am I talking about? Here again I want you to step back and look at the world around you. Do you just accept the culture that surrounds you? Think about that for a minute. In most cases, folks just do as their neighbors, friends, and family members do. Is that you? Go ahead and pull up a chair, I have another story to tell that should help in understanding why it is we must challenge the world in which we live.

Once upon a time, there was a young man who was surrounded by a culture of ignorance and "right thinking" people. However, this kid chose to reject much of his culture. Don't fool yourself; this was a very difficult thing for him to do. Almost all of the people around him thought a certain way and behaved a certain way, and they expected others to do the same. This young man said no, and he decided to walk his own path. He slowly but surely educated himself, even though few around him encouraged such "crazy" behavior.

This young man overcame great obstacles, including his mother dying when he was just a child. Obstacles exist in everyone's life. This young man would not let these difficulties defeat him and his future. He had plans, and he would not be stopped.

This young man received very little formal education. He had to learn outside the classroom. He found his education through books, which told a different story than what he saw in his daily life.

This young man grew up to battle the world on important issues that would include slavery and keeping the United States of America from breaking up into tiny little pieces. Who was this great man? I am talking about Abraham Lincoln. President Lincoln challenged the culture in which he lived and, in turn, he played a big part in changing the world.

We live in a materialistic culture that promotes the idea that happiness can be attained simply by earning more and more money so you can acquire more and more stuff. Look around you, what do you see? I see millions of people chasing a vision of success that only exists in advertising. Yes, advertising that is full of beautiful people who make stuff look wonderful, exciting, and utterly amazing. We can learn a lesson from Abraham Lincoln.

President Lincoln set out to educate himself when the culture around him said, *don't bother.* Abraham Lincoln was determined to deal with the wrongs of slavery when others said, *they are not equal.* Abraham Lincoln created his own culture based on his own values, and so can you.

You and I know who Abraham Lincoln was. How about the people and culture that surrounded him during his time growing up in Kentucky and Indiana? Dare to challenge the world around you. Educate yourself beyond the classroom and beyond what you can see in your current environment. Be the creator of your life!

People are always blaming their circumstances for what they are. I don't believe in circumstances. The people who get on in this world are the people who get up and look for the circumstances they want, and, if they can't find them, make them.

- **George Bernard Shaw**

12

INSIDE OUT

Our culture has, over time, changed in some very big ways. "Fixing" yourself on the outside is one of them. We are told that success and happiness comes to people who buy beautiful clothing, lovely accessories, shiny new cars, and very large and opulent homes. That is a lie and you should reject it.

Happiness comes from within. It comes from inside you and then radiates outward through your language, attitudes, and behaviors. This is not a new concept. I certainly did not come up with it all by myself. As a matter of fact, I had to learn about this thing called happiness.

Over the years, I came to realize that if I really wanted to be happy and truly fulfilled as a human being, there was nothing external that was going to do that for me. It had to be internal, not external. It had to come from understanding exactly who I am and what was truly going to bring me inner peace, "success," and happiness.

Notice the quotations around success. That word is subjective and, sadly, in many societies today, we define that word by the accumulation of more money and more stuff. This may include things like designer clothing, diamonds, new cars, and large and expensive homes.

In many cases, we tend to define success from the view of external changes in our environment. We are what we wear. We are what we drive. We are "somebody" based on the size of our bank account. Is this true? This is only true if you allow it to be true. Reject this approach to living your life.

Let's back up for a moment and look at the marketing campaigns that work at convincing you to buy the stuff that will make you "happy" and more "successful." This of course is a way of fixing you from the outside in. It doesn't work. It never has, and it never will. Reject those external fixes.

Here are three wonderful books that can set you down that path of enlightenment: *The Simple Dollar* by Trent Hamm, *The High Price of Materialism* by Tim Kasser, and *Choosing Simplicity* by Linda Breen Pierce. These books can change the way you think, which in turn will change your behaviors and relationships with others. Make the investment in you by reading these books. You're worth it.

Here is a tip I have learned during my journey: Identify successful people and learn as much from them as you possibly can. Here is the rub, though. Too many people define success based on how much stuff they have relative to what other people may have. They use the same logic in regards to money. Many people define success based on the size of their bank account compared to others. That is a mistake

When I say successful people, I am referring to happy people who are not trapped by seeking external fixes to their life. They are done playing the game that cannot be won. They have learned how to become happy from the inside out.

As a single footstep will not make a path on the earth, so a single thought will not make a pathway in the mind. To make a deep physical path, we walk again and again. To make a deep mental path, we must think over and over the kind of thoughts we wish to dominate our lives.

- **Henry David Thoreau**

13

THE COMPUTER

I have another story to tell, so pour yourself a nice cool drink, sit back, and enjoy. Once upon a time, your humble author was introduced to his first computer. This little contraption was strange, new, and confusing to a young kid from small-town America. A buddy of mine had purchased it, and he was excited about showing it off to his friends. He was very passionate about this amazing device. I wasn't.

This machine seemed slow, it had a lot of weird green lettering on it, and I just did not get it. It looked like a big box of electronics that my friend had gotten suckered into buying. Whoops. Clearly I was no visionary when it came to the home computer. What is the point? There are a few that I would like to highlight.

Do not discount the future implications of what you are exposed to today. I basically ignored that first computer, and I clearly did not see the value of something revolutionary when it was right smack-dab in front of my eyes.

It was very shortsighted on my part to overlook the computer, which means I delayed my learning curve about computers by many years. That was a mistake, and I admit it. I failed to see or consider what could be when it came to the personal home computer.

You may not see the value of this "money stuff" today. You will one day. Just keep an open mind as you are presented new information that seems strange and foreign to you. Something I should have done way back then when it came to that strange looking contraption called a computer.

When we are presented something new and "out there," we have a tendency to pull back and discount it. This is exactly how I responded to that first computer. I should not have been so quick to condemn something I did not understand.

My final point is a simple one. You don't finish a marathon without running the first mile. Just because I was unable to see all the possibilities that came with that first computer doesn't mean I should have shrugged it off as meaningless or not worth my time.

You are not going to become a financial genius by reading one book on personal finance. Your education, language, attitudes, and behaviors will evolve as you develop the right habits and get rid of the wrong ones. This really is a journey.

You need patience as you develop those habits and an open mind as you go forth on this passage of financial enlightenment. Yes, you read that right. This is more than just an education we are seeking. We are reaching for something even more important that will open up worlds that we may not even know exists. Onward!

Your time is limited, so don't waste it living someone else's life. Don't be trapped by dogma—which is living with the results of other people's thinking. Don't let the noise of others' opinions drown out your own inner voice. And most important, have the courage to follow your heart and intuition.

- **Steve Jobs**

14

CHALLENGES AHEAD

Do you think anyone gets to go through life without facing difficult obstacles? Do you think some people are just lucky, and that is why they are successful? I hope you answered no to each of those questions. The reality is this: We all will have many obstacles to overcome in our lives.

Some folks will have bigger challenges than others. That's life, and it's not fair much of the time. The real question is this: How will you react to the obstacles in your life? This one question, and how you answer it, will tell us a great deal about your future. Your answer will also have a big impact on your finances.

Financial achievement is not easy. While I would tell you that it is relatively simple, I would never say it is easy. If it were easy, everyone would do it, and you probably would not be reading this book. I am sure there will be many difficult obstacles in your path as you reach for financial happine$$. Expect the obstacles, and don't let them stop you or impede you on your journey.

Maybe you were born dirt poor. Maybe you were neglected or ignored as a child. Maybe your dad or mom told you how insignificant you were as you were finding your way in life. Maybe people discriminated against you because you were the wrong color, the wrong religion, the wrong size, the wrong sex, maybe just the wrong person.

There are many obstacles that confront us on a daily basis, and that is not going to change anytime soon. The question still remains: How will you react to the obstacles that come into your life?

As we look at the truly successful in life, belief in one's abilities, persistence, self-sufficiency and a disciplined focus on what was critically important seem to be present in almost all cases. You must acquire the mentality of a person who will persevere, because you believe you are worth it. Be tenacious!

You must deal with obstacles as if they were challenges, not roadblocks. You must see opportunity where others see stop signs. You must recognize that your attitude will get you far in life, and realize that an optimistic, pleasant personality will bring you into the company of other optimistic, pleasant people. Finally, you grasp the idea that wealth is built over a lifetime through the proper attitudes, behaviors, and habits that lead you down the right path while avoiding the wrong paths.

Have you heard of Helen Keller? What about Thomas Edison? Let's not forget Abraham Lincoln. These three amazing people were not born great people. Their journey in life made them great. They did not let obstacles stop them (they had many).

Overcoming obstacles made these people great. They overcame the difficulties in their lives and then set out to help others. This is something you and I can do as well.

Live YOUR dreams. Take the time to figure out what your dream is (make sure it is your dream and not someone else's), identify the obstacles in your way, draw up a plan, and do it! Success comes to those who get up when they get knocked down. Get up!

We need to give each other the space to grow, to be ourselves, to exercise our diversity. We need to give each other space so that we may both give and receive such beautiful things as ideas, openness, dignity, joy, healing, and inclusion.

- **Max de Pree**

15

THE BOOK

A good book can change the direction of your life. I would like to pause and go back to 1989, the point where my journey began. I found myself searching for answers in a rather small bookstore on Ledward Barracks in Schweinfurt, Germany, on a rather normal day in my military life. I was seeking help, but what kind of help, I had no clue. As I mentioned before, I spotted a book written by Charles Givens, *Wealth Without Risk*. That book transformed the way I thought and acted when it came to money.

Even though I only understood a small amount of the book at the time, the light bulb was turned on in my head. I started to read more books on finance, and then I read the Givens book again. This time, I understood much more of the book and the overarching message.

Actually, I came up with even more questions about this "new world" I was seeing and learning about. I even took a week off and spent my vacation holed up in my apartment, reading more books. I know it sounds like a strange way to spend a vacation, but it turned out to be one of the most important weeks of my life.

I learned there was a financial world that I had not known existed. *Wealth Without Risk* was my first step on a long financial literacy journey. I can assure you that book has changed my life, and not only in monetary terms. More importantly, it gave me the confidence in my abilities to change other aspects of my life. That is the power of a book.

Whether you read a book by flipping the pages (old school) or electronically on some of the new devices, just do it. Maybe you will choose to purchase an audio book on finance and listen to it during your morning commute. Perhaps you will find some creative way to use your smart phone during a break in your busy schedule. Your options are endless, but you must do something, anything, to increase your knowledge about personal finance and how it all works. Books open up worlds we have yet to see or know exist. It's worth your time to explore the unknown.

Which book is right for you? Only you can know the answer to that question, and that means you must read books written by different authors who will provide you with unique ways of thinking and living in this crazy world we have created. This idea is called comparative reading. Simply identify authors presenting different perspectives, and spend the time looking at life from those different angles. Some very wise people are ready to share what they know. I have shared some of my favorites in the back of this book in Appendix A. Try a few out.

The reason I reached my goals had very little to do with my job, how much money I made, my formal education, or even my intelligence. It had a great deal to do with gathering a financial and academic education outside the classroom and then acting on what I had learned.

I found my teachers in books, and so can you. Turn the television off, cancel the shopping trip to the mall, and pick up a book; your world will never be the same.

Books were my pass to personal freedom. I learned to read at age three, and soon discovered there was a whole world to conquer that went beyond our farm in Mississippi.

- **Oprah Winfrey**

16

THE CITY LIMITS

I have another interesting story to share. It involves a wise old woman, a couple of newcomers, and the world we have created for ourselves.

Once upon a time there was a newcomer who decided to move to a new city, and as he reached the city limits he came upon a wise old woman sitting by the road. The newcomer asked the old woman what the people in this new city were like. The old woman asked the newcomer, "What were the people like in the city you just left?"

The newcomer said they were a bunch of no-good, crooked, rotten, deceitful creatures, and he was glad to leave them behind. The wise old woman told the newcomer he would find the same type of people in this new city. The newcomer was not happy about this news. He waved the old woman off as he proceeded into his new town, kicking a stray dog along the way.

The next day another newcomer approached the same wise old woman on the outskirts of the same city. Just as the previous newcomer had done, he asked the old woman what the people were like in this new city. The wise old woman responded with the same question. "What were the people like in the city you just left?"

The newcomer described how beautiful, honest, decent, and giving the people were in his previous city. The wise old woman told the newcomer he would find the same type of people in this new city. With that, the newcomer proceeded on with some pep in his step and a smile on his face.

How can two people experience the same thing, and yet have two totally separate views on an experience? *Life tends to play out around us in large part based on what is within us.* Why is it that some people seem to have a gift that brings out the best in others, and some do the opposite? The answer lies with you. What you do and how you act greatly affects how others respond to you.

The world you see is the world you have created. Do you like what you see? Do you like the people in your city? Are you counting the days when you can move to a "better" city with "better" people?

Are you familiar with the law of attraction? You will very likely attract people who are similar to you in thought and behavior. If you want the right kind of people to enter your life, be the right kind of person.

How you handle the money that comes into your life will have a big impact on the relationships you have with others. A person who is mired in debt and stress tends to see the world from a victim's viewpoint. This causes the debtor to see others as the enemy, and this will feed his fear and contempt of others. On the other hand, the saver/investor will see his fellow citizens as potential friends and as fellow travelers on this roller coaster journey we call life.

Choose your city.

We are shaped by our thoughts; we become what we think. When the mind is pure, joy follows like a shadow that never leaves.

- **The Buddha**

17

CAN YOU CHANGE?

How open are you to change? Many people fight change, even when it clearly can help them. Why? I have another sad but true story to tell, and I am afraid lives were lost because of the unwillingness of decent and intelligent men to change and adapt to new information. After you read this story, please take a moment to reflect on your willingness to change when new information is presented to you.

James Lind, a British naval surgeon, published a book in the 1700's in which he identified how scurvy could be eliminated simply by supplying sailors with lemon juice. He cited many case histories from his experience as a naval surgeon, and he proved that such things as mustard cress, tamarinds, oranges, and lemons would prevent scurvy. (These things are chock-full of vitamin C.) You would think Dr. Lind would have been praised for this great contribution, right? He was ridiculed. In fact, the Lords of the Admiralty and other physicians ignored Dr. Lind's advice for many decades. He was deemed "crazy."

One sea captain did take his advice: Captain James Cook. Captain Cook stocked his ships with plenty of fresh fruit. The Royal Society honored Captain Cook in 1776 for his success in eliminating scurvy, but yet, the officials of the navy continued to ignore Dr. Lind's report.

Not until 1794 was a British navy squadron supplied with lemon juice before a voyage. That voyage lasted twenty-three weeks resulting in no single case of scurvy. It took forty years before Dr. Lind's research was used to save the lives of sailors around the world. Yes, forty years! All it took was a few lemons and an open mind, and yet educated men ignored this information. 3

So why do I tell this story? Time and again, wise men and women from our past have provided us with financial advice that can truly change our lives, but how many of us heed this information? It's one thing to say you are open to change; it's something else to actually act upon what you have learned.

There is a path one can use to create wealth, obtain freedom, live your dreams, and find true and long-lasting happiness. That path is real. I promise to show you some strange ways of looking at the world as we proceed forward. This will require a new way of thinking and behaving. Are you ready?

Here is a brief story that may help explain this point even further. Two computer salespeople were sent to an isolated community in the middle of nowhere to sell computers. A few weeks passed, and both salespeople were due to report their status to the home office. The first one calls in and says, "I'm coming back; no one here uses a computer." The second one calls in and says, "I will be here a long time; no one here uses a computer!" Which one are you?

The most valuable thing you can ever own is your image of yourself as a winner in the great game of life, as a contributor to the betterment of humankind, as an achiever of worthy goals. Unless you have that image of yourself, nothing worth having will stay with you for long.

- **Tom Hopkins,** *The Official Guide to Success*

18

MIKE FINLEY, CMPW

How many financial experts do you know with all those impressive initials after their name? Did you know I have some mighty important letters after my name? For years now I have been certified as Mike Finley, CMPW (Crazy Man in the Pink Wig). I proudly distinguish myself by my initials and my rather identifiable pink wig. Why?

The pink wig represents my personal commitment to my financial life. What? Yes, when I wear my pink wig, I am telling the world that I am the answer when it comes to determining how my life unfolds. Now, I know many of you are thinking, *this man has lost his marbles*. Maybe.

The pink wig is a symbol of something very important, and it is significant to know there are even deeper meanings as we delve into this rather odd image (meanings only you can "see" once you accept personal responsibility for your financial life and then act on them).

I want you to challenge what you think you know. Maybe all those beautiful images you see (advertising) are not so real. Maybe all those people driving brand new cars and wearing beautiful designer clothing are not so wealthy. Maybe all those professionals (financial industry helpers) are not so wise.

Financial literacy provides you with knowledge on a wide variety of subjects, such as how to wisely use credit, how to smartly buy a vehicle and a home, where to invest, where not to invest, and what to invest in, all of which in turn empowers you to make better decisions with your money. Financial literacy will not only help you make good decisions, but it will also help you avoid making bad decisions.

To wear the pink wig proudly is a sign that you have fully accepted the message. It says, "I am willing to stand my ground, even if I stick out from the crowd. I don't want to be part of the crowd. The crowd is living paycheck to paycheck, stressed out and broke!"

Financial literacy can bring freedom and, ultimately, happiness into your life. The credentials behind my name can be the credentials behind your name. What is crazier, being financially free and wearing a pink wig, or being financially ignorant with mounds of debt, no savings, and the stress that accompanies these things?

Here is a message I need you to hear: You have every right to reject a culture that does not serve your needs and, on a deeper level, your soul. You can create your own culture. You can allow the environment to change you or you can change the environment. This is the overarching message behind the "crazy" man in the pink wig. The power lies with YOU!

The CMPW can be modified to CWPW (Crazy Woman in the Pink Wig) or how about CKPW (Crazy Kid in the Pink Wig)? What about CGPW (Crazy Grandparent in the Pink Wig)? Use your creativity and your courage as you join me on this unusual journey into craziness. You can wear the pink wig anywhere (your shirt, your jeans, your jacket, and yes, even on your head). Join me!

Believe in yourself! Have faith in your abilities! Without a humble but reasonable confidence in your own powers you cannot be successful or happy.

- **Norman Vincent Peale**

19

HIS NAME WAS JACK

Do you know who Jack LaLanne was? If not, you will learn a bit in the following pages, and you can learn more with a simple Google search as you explore this truly amazing man. Jack LaLanne was born in 1914 and, sadly, he passed away in January 2011, after a long and illustrious career. Some of you may know Jack as the "juicer guy," but there was a great deal more to this man.

Jack became a convert to the world of fitness in his teens, and in the 1930s he opened one of the first fitness gyms in the United States. *Few people came.* In 1951, Jack started and funded his own television show, teaching people about the value of fitness and a proper diet. *Most people tuned him out.* It took years before folks started to pay attention. Finally, a major network picked up his show in 1959, and millions of people were exposed to this "crazy" man in a tight jumpsuit doing exercises and preaching healthy living. Jack was changing his environment even though the people in his environment were not ready to change.

Many people questioned the sanity of this man, but now as we look back in time, Jack appears to be quite sane performing all of his exercises in his very revealing outfit. To the amazement of millions, he even included his wife in the workouts. Shocking!

Jack knew what he was doing, and he knew it was the right thing to do at the right time. If others weren't ready for this "crazy" way of thinking and living, well then so be it. He was ready, and he was going to lead the way. 4

Jack LaLanne died at the age of ninety-six of pneumonia. He was a shining example to us all in the way in which he lived his life. He showed us the power of one person and what a person can do when properly motivated by their passion. You can be that person.

The world today is full of people who spend more than they make. They buy stuff with their credit cards even though they do not have the money in the bank to pay for it. They save little or nothing, because most of their money is going toward consumable products that will be worth almost nothing very soon.

The crowd lives paycheck to paycheck because *that is just the way you do it.* The crowd accepts their fate, and they see no way to escape it. The crowd accepts the belief that they are victims. None of these thoughts or actions will serve a person well, that I can promise you. I wonder what Jack would say about this type of self-destructive behavior?

Here is my best guess: Get your act together. You can do this. Get started with your financial education, and start doing what is right for you and your family. If you have to work three jobs, then you work three jobs. If you have to cut spending, then you cut spending. You do what you have to do. You can do this. Follow me.

Jack did not accept the status quo. He created his own world, and so can you if you are willing to leave the safety of the crowd. It's time to live YOUR dreams and not someone else's. It's time to find YOU.

Follow the path of the unsafe, independent thinker. Expose your ideas to the danger of controversy. Speak your mind and fear less the label of "crackpot" than the stigma of conformity.

- **Thomas John Watson, Sr.**

Stage II

TRAVELLING FROM HERE TO THERE

20

JUDGMENT DAY

Here is one of those ideas that, if you apply it, can dramatically change the direction of your financial life. This concept will require a decent amount of labor and self-discipline on your part, but I know you are ready for it at this point in your journey. You are ready to change the way you think about money, and that means you are ready to change the way you handle the money that comes into your life.

Judgment day is the day you go through every single financial piece of your life. I mean EVERYTHING. Why would I ask you to do such a tedious task?

If you have a few years under your belt, you know that it is easy to get a little careless when it comes to spending money here and there. Gradually, over time, these things add up until finally you have reached a point where you are wasting hundreds, if not thousands, of dollars each and every month. Judgment day can put a halt to this type of behavior as you start to gain control of your financial life.

Do I really mean EVERYTHING? Yes, I mean every single financial item in your life. Go through your finances and break down everything that deals with your money. Pull out your paystub, and review your income, the taxes withheld, your insurance, your food bills, your credit cards, your utilities, everything.

If it deals with money, account for it. Is this a pain in the butt? Yes. Will this take a few hours? Yes. Can this cause tension within your family? YES! Again, the question comes down to why? You want something greater than you currently have, and I am not talking about more stuff.

Judgment day can change the course of your life. It should cause you to begin asking questions. What is that tax for? Why do we pay that much? Why is that coming out of my paycheck? I thought we cancelled that. It is time to take charge of your finances and rid yourself of the waste that has become part of your life.

It is time to make this extraordinary effort for something greater. Freedom! Yes, the kind of freedom that comes to someone who values his/her time and money. *Your Money or Your Life* by Vicki Robin and Joe Dominguez can help you with this very important concept. There is a path that can lead to financial happine$$, and it is a path worth taking. It's time to get on that path.

All of the money you free up can be used to pay down debt, increase savings, and provide you more opportunities than you ever imagined as you go forward with your future.

Once you identify something specific as a priority in your life, you are well on your way toward accomplishing it. Make judgment day a priority as you set forth on a journey of financial discovery and personal enlightenment. Just do it.

I have completed this task more than once in my life when I found myself getting lazy in my spending. When I say lazy, I mean wasting my money on stuff that brought little value to my life. To be lazy is to be human. Overcoming those feelings requires self-discipline and the belief in your ability to change. This is your opportunity!

I am free because I know that I alone am morally responsible for everything I do. I am free, no matter what rules surround me. If I find them tolerable, I tolerate them; if I find them too obnoxious, I break them.

- **Robert A. Heinlein**

21

DO YOU USE THE B WORD?

Well, do you? You know, the word that causes so many people to cringe when they hear it. You know, "budget." Do you have a budget? Here is the answer I get more times than not when I ask that question. *Sort of.* Is that your answer? Well, I have some good news, and I have some not so good news. You *sort of* have a chance at a successful financial life when you fail to account for the money you have coming in and going out of your life. *Sort of* is not going to cut it.

It is time to take control of your life and start tracking your spending. A simple tracking system will help you budget your money effectively, which will in turn help you save and invest for your long-term goals, such as buying a home, saving for college, or maybe that wonderful thing called retirement.

Budgeting seems to put many people on the defensive. They feel controlled. A budget can feel like your money is controlling you rather than you controlling it. I get that, and that is why I want you to track your money first. What is the difference?

A budget says you can only spend so much on this and so much on that, and if you go over then shame on you. No wonder so few people budget. Tracking where your money is spent is a different approach that should help in developing a budget in a gradual and self-reflective way. The key is to identify a simple and sustainable system that you can consistently follow month after month and year after year.

Tracking your spending shows you where your money is going and for what purpose. You MUST do this. I am not here to tell you what you should spend your money on. That is up to you based on your values, goals, and priorities. However, I do want you to track your expenses so you can identify the value of those purchases.

How? Use one method of payment. For most people this could be a debit card or a credit card. Make all your purchases with that one card, and then print off the statement at the end of the month. Next, you place your spending into categories, and then put the numbers on your spreadsheet that you update each and every month. You can use cash as well, but be vigilant about writing down each and every purchase. You will need a pad and pen readily available when tracking cash purchases.

At the end of the month, review your tracking document and ask yourself some questions. Do I need this? Does this help me to reach my goals? Was my spending in line with my values? Without a simple system of tracking, you really have no shot at answering these valuable questions.

You do not need an accounting degree, or any degree at all for that matter, to track your money. Go to thecrazymaninthepinkwig.com and download the "tracking your spending" spreadsheet to help you identify where your money is going. Mint.com and powerwallet.com are also options you may consider. Make it happen!

Your vision will become clear only when you can look into your own heart. Who looks outside, dreams; who looks inside, awakes.

\- **Carl Jung**

22

WHAT ARE YOU WORTH?

The net-worth statement is a critical piece of any financial plan. This document shows where you currently are financially. It should be completed at least once each calendar year.

Many people (based on research done by Thomas Stanley as he studied millionaires and the ones who want to be) gauge their financial success by how much money they make or by how much stuff they have accumulated in the house or the garage. That is a mistake that will cost you dearly far beyond just money.

There are plenty of high-income people with plenty of stuff who are broke! Again, it is not how much you make, but how much you end up keeping that really makes a difference in your financial life.

The net-worth statement shows you what you are worth financially based on your assets and liabilities. It is very important that you use this document to figure out where you are financially and then track your progress throughout the years and decades. Now let's take a look at some of the explanations people make as they describe why they fail to complete this form on a yearly basis.

I am not an accountant. Neither am I, so what? *Businesses must do this, not individuals.* That would be dead wrong. *No one ever showed me how.* I am showing you now. *I do not know how.* I have provided a template on my website with simple instructions. *I don't have time.* Make time; this is important. *I am poor.* You do not know just how poor you are until you complete the form. *I make a lot of money, so I don't need to do this.* The bankruptcy courts are full of people who made a lot of money.

Did I miss anything? You need to track what you are doing so you know whether you are going in the right direction or the wrong direction financially. *Think back to my situation as a young adult and how surprised I was when I found out which direction I was heading.* Now let's look at a few specifics before you get started.

I want you to identify the value of all of your assets and categorize who you owe and how much you owe. It will take some effort as you track down all of your money and the value of your property. It's worth your time, I promise you.

I have provided what I would say is an ugly net-worth statement as well as a good net-worth statement at thecrazymaninthepinkwig.com. Hit on the *Net Worth* tab and copy and paste this document onto your computer.

Once you have completed the research on your assets and liabilities, simply put them down on the spreadsheet with their estimated value. I have already completed the formulas that will add and subtract for you. Put your numbers in, and then let the spreadsheet do the rest.

Do not beat yourself up if it looks ugly right now. My first one looked ugly too. This is where you are starting, not where you are ending. The journey begins when we start. Start now!

It is true that I am fundamentally an optimist, that I am congenitally hopeful. I do not believe that good always conquers evil, because I have lived a long time in the world and seen that it is not true... It is not wishful thinking that makes me a hopeful woman. Over and over, I have seen, under the most improbable circumstances, that man can remake himself, that he can even remake his world if he cares enough to try.

- **Eleanor Roosevelt,** *You Learn by Living*

23

REACH FOR THE SKY!

One of the best ways to achieve financial happine$$ is by setting challenging, but realistic, goals that make up your financial plan. This means more than just dreaming about it. Write down your short and long-term goals, and then hold yourself responsible for meeting those goals. (There is an example with instructions on my website). Let's take a look at some very specific goals that one could select. Focus on making your goals as specific as possible, as this will improve your chances of achieving them.

- Put $200 per month into a Roth IRA that will shelter my total stock market index fund from taxes starting January 1.

- Raise my 401(k) contributions by 2 percent starting on January 1.

- Start tracking every dollar I spend. I will add up the money spent at the end of the month and place it on a spreadsheet for my review. Develop a budget after two months of review.

- Double my car payment each month.

- Read *Personal Finance for Dummies* in the first half of the year and *The Little Book of Commonsense Investing* in the second half of the year.

- Start a 529 Plan for college at vanguard.com, and put $100 in the 500 index fund every month for my one-year-old son.

- Get quotes from multiple sources on all my insurance policies as I focus on getting the best value for my money.

- Make an extra $100 payment to my mortgage principal every month. I will build equity and reduce how much interest I pay.

- Take fewer trips in my car. Keep lists that help me track what I need so I can save money on gas.

- Pay off my credit cards in full each and every month. Request a credit limit increase even though I don't need it. This will increase my credit score without taking on more credit.

- Get married in December. My savings will cover the cost of the wedding and the rings. I will go on my honeymoon debt free!

- Pay off my entire debt in three years. Write my debts down, and pay the smallest ones off first while working up to the biggest ones. Cut out the extra stuff until I get this done.

- Save $500 each month in a Short-Term Bond Index Fund at vanguard.com, and buy a home in four years.

Goals keep us focused. Your financial future is a blank slate waiting to be filled. Fill it in with your goals, which are nothing more than dreams written down. Achieving your goals will help you achieve your dreams. Believe it!

What you get by achieving your goals is not as important as what you become by achieving your goals.

- **Henry David Thoreau**

24

MONEY DAY

Pick one day out of the year, and make that your money day. What is money day? That is the day you review your entire financial situation as you prepare a plan for your financial future.

There should be a list of things you complete on this day. As noted earlier, I have provided you with examples of a tracking document, a net-worth statement, and a financial plan at thecrazymaninthepinkwig.com.

I would recommend allotting an entire morning or evening to this endeavor. Now I know some of you are saying to yourself, *that's just great; when I find the time, I'll let you know*! Let's take a moment and consider what I am asking you to do. I want you to take a few hours out of the YEAR to evaluate your financial situation. Make the time. Don't be an ostrich.

- Update the *Tracking Spreadsheet*: See where your money is going.

- Complete a *Net-Worth Statement*: Identify where you are financially.

- Evaluate your *Insurance Policies*: Review them carefully for need based on value, and review your deductibles, raising them when possible (this will lower your yearly premiums).

- Check your *Credit Reports and Credit Scores*: Review them for errors or outdated information; details on this are covered later in the book. This one step alone can save you thousands of dollars over your lifetime.

- Update your *Financial Plan*. This is where you place your short- and long-term goals on paper as you plan and prepare for a future of your choosing.

Okay, so you concede that this is important, so now what? Save each of the documents from my website to your home computer, place your numbers in the appropriate blocks, and *presto*, you have yourself a real start toward completing money day. This can be done and it should be done. It all comes down to you and how willing you are to make changes in your financial life. Schedule it, prepare for it, and get it done.

Once you have completed money day, hold that person in the mirror accountable. Money day is a critical component toward getting control of your financial life. Complete it at least once each year as your life unfolds over time. I would encourage you to review the previous year prior to starting your money day. You may be surprised by what you see.

Write everything down, make changes as needed, file the paperwork in a safe place when you're done, and refer to it periodically during the year as you work at achieving the goals you have set. Taking control of your money means taking action with what you have learned. Do it!

No matter how dramatic the end result, the good-to-great transformations never happened in one fell swoop. There was no single defining action, no grand program, no one killer innovation, no solitary lucky break, no miracle moment. Rather, the process resembled relentlessly pushing a giant heavy flywheel in one direction, turn upon turn, building momentum until a point of breakthrough, and beyond.

- **Jim Collins**, *Good to Great*

25

OWN THE RIGHT ASSETS

If you want to have more control over your financial life, I would encourage you to own appreciating assets that grow over time. (They gradually go up in value, even with a few bad years along the way.) Here is a small, but very important, list of *appreciating assets* available to the average person. Buy them with great care. You can lose money with any one of these types of assets. Evaluate each investment based on what it earns after cost. *After* is the key word here.

- *Own a business*: Identify your passion and spend your life living it. Chase your passion and the money will come. Chase after money and you may end up with nothing.

- *Own stocks*: Specifically, own passively managed no-load index mutual funds.

- *Own bonds*: Same advice. Own passively managed no-load index mutual funds.

- *Own your own home*: Wisely select one you can afford based on value and comfort, while monitoring costs very carefully. This is a good asset to own only if you own it for a very long time.

- *Own rental property*: This can include rental real estate or passively managed no-load REIT index mutual funds that own stock in publicly held commercial real estate.

You will notice that just owning is not good enough, you must own *wisely*, which means you are focused on upfront and recurring costs. Now let's take a look at a few *depreciating assets* that will gradually make your poorer over time.

- *A car or truck*: Automobiles lose a great deal of value over time (especially new vehicles) with high recurring costs. Vehicles are one of the most wealth depleting assets you can own.

- *Clothing*: Clothing loses almost all of its value immediately with low to moderate recurring costs over time.

- *Furniture*: Furniture loses much of its value in a short period of time with generally low recurring costs.

- *Toys*: This list may include jet skis, boats, golf clubs, televisions, computers, cell phones, etc. These items lose considerable value over time with generally high recurring costs.

The future wealthy will gradually build wealth over time as they purchase the first group of appreciating assets, while limiting how much they spend on the wealth depleting depreciating assets. The choice is clear if you desire financial freedom in your future.

Don't let the opinions of the average man sway you. Dream, and he thinks your crazy. Succeed, and he thinks your lucky. Acquire wealth, and he thinks your greedy. Pay no attention. He simply doesn't understand.

- Robert G. Allen

Stage III

MISTAKES YOU MUST AVOID

26

CRATERS

If you are ever going to accumulate wealth, which will provide you the financial freedom to live the life of your dreams, you must avoid the financial craters that are in your path.

Numerous times over the years, I have been asked, *what is the best investment?* I respond with an answer that generally receives a rather lukewarm reaction. The best investment is an investment in YOU. It always has been, and it always will be. Becoming financially literate will provide you with the education that will help you avoid the craters in life, and there are some very deep craters.

I would like to take a moment to help you visualize your path to wealth and financial freedom. It is a long road that seems to go on forever. All along the path, there are craters that stand in your way. You must keep your eyes wide open and be very careful; otherwise you will certainly fall into one of these very large and deep holes. If this happens, it will take a great deal of time, money, and effort to find your way out.

Some craters are so deep that you will need help from family, friends, and possibly professionals, just to get out. When you lack financial literacy, you are wearing a blindfold as you maneuver your way along your journey of life.

Blindfolds will cripple your financial future as you fall into one crater after another. This must be avoided if you want something better for you and your family. The blindfold must go, and you're the one in charge of taking it off. It all comes down to you and what you are going to do based on what you have learned.

When we send kids out into the world with nothing more than a checking account and a pat on the head, we are actually placing a blindfold on them and saying, *good luck!* They don't stand a chance unless that blindfold is taken off and they are given the opportunity to see where they are going and how they can avoid the craters in life. Let me state the obvious: Craters are much easier to see when we know where to look.

Here is a small sample of common craters: making minimum payments on a credit card, valuing who you are according to the stuff you own, trying to get rich fast with nothing down and no risk, believing and following the messages you receive in those daily advertisements, trusting commission-based salespeople in the financial industry, buying new cars as often as possible, and finally, spending your free time shopping for the next "great" thing.

How do I know about these craters? Initially, I learned the hard way, by falling into my own set of craters, and let me tell you, some were mighty deep. It took my time, it took my money, and it caused me a decent amount of pain and agony before I was able to climb out of those craters. Avoid the craters!

I was fortunate. I saw the path and found my way toward financial literacy, but I needed help. I am sure most of you have heard the old saying, *you can learn the easy way or you can learn the hard way.* Falling into these craters is time-consuming and exhausting. Don't learn the hard way.

Happiness is not something ready made. It comes from your own actions.

- **Dalai Lama**

27

HOW TO BECOME BROKE

We are inundated with news stories about becoming rich and famous. What do you say we try a different approach? How about identifying how to become broke? Everything on the list below should go a long way toward helping you do just that. Hang on, because this will not be pretty nor will it be pleasant. Sometimes the truth hurts.

- Never read a book on personal finance.

- Run up your credit cards and make the minimum payments whenever possible.

- Take out as many school loans as you can, and then take a lifetime to pay them back.

- Live paycheck to paycheck, and don't worry about saving money. Live for today, that's all that matters.

- Play the lottery as often as possible. While you're at it, hit the casino!

- Spend your time getting payday loans, renting your stuff, and pawning your "valuables." Own nothing.

- Make shopping one of your favorite activities.

- Find get-rich-quick schemes and invest NOW!

- Buy a new car as often as possible. While you're at it, don't do any research before buying.
- Base your self-esteem on what you wear, where you live, and what you drive.
- Blame others for your problems in life. Repeat after me: *I am a victim.*
- Don't worry about your total debt. Focus solely on the monthly payment.
- Buy the biggest wedding and the biggest ring so everyone can see just how fabulous you really are.
- Work at a job you hate, and spend your free time buying happiness.
- Treat those "amazing" celebrities and "successful" athletes as role models. Try to be just like them whenever possible.
- When you come into some free money, spend it.
- Make the appearance of wealth one of your top priorities as you focus on acquiring more stuff.
- Stop your education when someone hands you a diploma.

I don't think of myself as a poor deprived ghetto girl who made good. I think of myself as somebody who from an early age knew I had to make good.

- **Oprah Winfrey**

28

DINNER, ANYONE?

It is always fun to have lunch or dinner out with family and friends. When done on an infrequent basis, it certainly can be a nice change of pace and a good opportunity to spend time with people you care about. The problem comes with the frequency of those meals eaten outside the home.

How often do you eat out at restaurants? If you are like many people, you either don't really keep track or you dramatically underestimate just how often and how much you spend on this convenient luxury. The key word here is *luxury*. This could be costing you thousands of dollars every year—dollars that could be better used elsewhere.

Now as I write this, I am quite certain many of you are shaking your head and wagging your finger at me. I just don't understand your busy life. I don't understand how difficult it is to get everything done while still finding time to feed yourself and your family. You're right. I don't know how busy your life is, but I do know how expensive it can be to eat outside the home repeatedly.

I am not here to chide you for eating out. I am not here to criticize your lifestyle. What I do want to point out is that life is full of choices. If you choose to spend a good chunk of your income eating out instead of saving it for future needs (which may include children, emergencies, retirement, and college), that is YOUR decision.

Life is full of trade-offs. Saving money for future needs versus eating out is one of those trade-offs. If you do not want to modify your restaurant habits, you can stop reading this chapter. As for the rest of you, let's move on.

Before we identify an approach that will help curb your spending on meals outside the home, let's review just how much it is actually costing you. First, the meal is going to run you around 7 percent extra, depending on your location, because of sales tax (sales tax varies based on location). Next, we need to tack on the tip, which will run at least 15 percent (18 percent in many places). Finally, we need to add the cost of overhead that the restaurant bakes into the prices so they can pay their staff and make a profit. This could easily add 50 percent to the cost of food you could have purchased at your local grocer (most places impose no sales tax on groceries). Adding it all up comes to 72 percent (7 + 15 + 50). This estimated percentage is probably on the low end.

You could easily be paying 100 percent or more at those lovely restaurants above and beyond what you would pay at the local grocer. Now let's look at ways to reduce these costs.

Pay in cash when you go out to eat. This one strategy will alert you to the reality of just how much money it is costing you to eat out. Another strategy is to set a specific amount of money per month that you allow yourself to spend on eating out. Let's say you have designated $200 per month as your allotted eating-out limit. When you reach that limit, you're done! Do not pass go, do not collect $100, you are done, period.

How do you stick to this limit without cheating? You have savings goals that are more important to you than eating out. This comes down to priorities. Identify them, and live them.

The individual has always had to struggle to keep from being overwhelmed by the tribe. If you try it, you will be lonely often, and sometimes frightened. But no price is too high to pay for the privilege of owning yourself.

- **Friedrich Nietzsche**

29

THE MACHINE

The machines will be running the world one day. Have you heard this statement before? I am here to tell you that machines are running the world *today*. It just may not be the machines you expected. Here I am talking about one very powerful machine; the massive marketing machine. This machine has been around a long time and continues to affect your life in ways you probably don't realize.

Some very persuasive people are manipulating your thinking, which in turn affects your day-to-day decision-making. The massive marketing machine is at the heart of this message. Not sure? Keep reading; let's see if I can convince you that all of your thinking is not really your thinking.

When I say manipulating, I mean brainwashing. I mean indoctrination. I mean those daily, weekly, monthly, and yearly advertising messages are changing how you feel, how you think, and how you ultimately behave. This is a fact ladies and gentlemen, and you need to know it before it's too late. Let's take a look.

I would like to ask you to take a break from your reading and do a mental walk-through of your home or apartment. With your mind, take a good hard look outside and inside your place (including the garage if you have one). How much stuff do you own that you barely if ever use or wear?

I challenge you to pick up a pad and pen and jot these items down as you come across them. How big of a list do you think you might have? If you are like many people, that list will be big and full of all kinds of stuff.

Let me tell you what I realized when I did this in my home: I had spent a great deal of money over the years on stuff that added little or nothing to my life. As I looked at these meaningless items, I paused to reflect on why I bought them. I considered what it was that prompted me to accumulate more and more and more. What did I come up with? The massive marketing machine had convinced me that possessions would bring me success, love, popularity, happiness, you name it.

Here is one book that explains this concept quite well: *Debt is Slavery and 9 Other Things I Wish My Dad Had Taught Me About Money*, by Michael Mihalik. This small book can help you see the world of marketing from a different perspective, a perspective that most companies would prefer you avoid. The massive marketing machine is alive and well in America and many places abroad. Beware; someone is planting ideas in your head.

What have I learned about this insidious machine? You must learn to modify your thinking and behaviors if you ever want to escape the reach of some very creative and clever marketing campaigns. The people behind those campaigns are very talented. Be aware of that when you start to think you are easily capable of ignoring their messages.

You can improve your financial situation by improving your self-esteem. By accepting and embracing who you truly are, you will stop buying stuff to make you feel better about yourself. Work on the inside, and the outside will take care of itself.

The things that really matter in life are not sold in stores. Love, friendship, family, respect, a place in the community, the belief that your life has purpose; those are the essentials of human fulfillment, and they cannot be purchased with cash. Everyone needs a certain amount of money, but chasing money rather than meaning is a formula for discontent.

- **Greg Easterbrook**

30

THE SALE!

There is something special about a sale, right? You feel as if you are getting a deal that would normally not be available. You are "saving" money as you spend it, thanks to the deep discount the business is providing you. You may think 50 percent off is great, and 75 percent off is amazing! Well, I want to offer you a sale at 107 percent off! Are you interested?

Many people react very favorably to a big sale. This is why you see them every day of the week, but you must buy NOW! It all sounds very familiar, doesn't it? Here is my question: Are you buying some item because you need it, or because it is such a great sale that you just cannot pass it up?

Take a moment and think about that loaded question. Those marketing geniuses know you better than you know you. I'm not exaggerating; they really do.

The marketing professionals know the emotional triggers that will open up your pocketbook, and convince you to let go of your money, and of course through the use of credit they get you to spend money you don't actually have. This technique is very effective, and it works—for THEM, not you.

You can get 107 percent off every sale available to man and woman if you simply do not buy the product that you do not need. (You will save 100 percent of the price of the item, as well as an estimated 7 percent in sales tax.) Let me say that once again. You can get 107 percent off if you do not fall for the marketing campaigns that are trying to get you to buy stuff right NOW!

I would like to challenge you a bit (as if I haven't already). For the next month, can you go without buying anything that is on sale? Go ahead and exempt your groceries, but that is all. I challenge you to avoid all sales for one month. This is a guaranteed way to get 107 percent off. Isn't that the deal of the century?

So what is the point of this lesson? You must delete that signal in your head that thinks you should buy because something is on sale. A sale is nothing more than a marketing tool used to get you into the store so you will buy not only the sale item, but also other items that are more lucrative for the business.

Putting items on sale works, which of course is why there is always a new sale popping up today, this week, and all the months to come. On a side note, don't fall for the "you will save a lot of money" approach. You are not saving money! You are spending money. They are simply using the word "save" in a way that will cause you to feel more positive about buying their product or service. Don't fall for it.

You must learn to ignore the concept of a sale when it comes to your everyday purchases. I want you to look at each sale that comes along and ask yourself: Is this something you need, or is this simply something you want based off the advertising pitch that has been presented to you repeatedly? Answer this question, and you will be far ahead of the crowd.

Identify those emotional triggers that cause you to plunk down money you may or may not have to buy stuff you probably don't need. Take control of YOU.

Advertising is the art of convincing people to spend what they don't have for something they don't need.
- **Will Rogers**

31

SNAKES ARE DANGEROUS!

Do you have credit card debt? I know some of you think there is nothing wrong with a little credit card debt. I disagree. Credit card debt may not literally kill you, but it can debilitate your life in many painful ways. It's kind of like a snake squeezing a poor field mouse that it captured during its hunt. It will end badly.

Credit card debt simply demonstrates that you are living beyond your means. There is no need to rationalize it. Do you have any savings? What is the interest rate on those savings? How much interest are you paying on your credit card(s)? Yes, now is the time to go look. It is absolutely crazy to have savings in the bank earning .2 percent while you pay 16 percent or more on your credit card debt. That is how you end up in the poor house.

Now I know that I may have hurt someone's feelings here. I am not saying you are dumb; I am saying what you are doing is irresponsible, which it is. Let's deal with the facts. By incurring credit card debt, you are sacrificing your future so you can live beyond your means today.

Credit card debt slowly strangles you. Month after month the interest adds up, and at some point you are shocked by what has happened. It reminds me of that poor mouse who gets swallowed by the deadly and powerful snake. The mouse slowly gets squeezed until it suffocates, and then it is swallowed. If you have credit card debt, you are that mouse. You are being squeezed and suffocated, and soon you will be swallowed (by bankruptcy and possibly home foreclosure).

You must fix the way you think long before you fix your finances. It is time to take action as you commit to ridding yourself of the credit card debt in your life. Save at least $500 (you might consider a couple of thousand to cover any deductibles on insurance policies) in a savings account, and then take everything else outside of retirement accounts, and PAY OFF YOUR CREDIT CARDS. This is also the time to sell anything that you do not need. Yes, that means going through the closet and the garage getting rid of stuff that is simply collecting dust. Now is the time to deal with this situation. Not tomorrow. *Now!*

Stop buying wants until your credit cards are paid off. Freeze those cards or cut them up if you must, but just stop with the madness of using credit cards to increase your standard of living beyond what it actually should be. Learning to live below your means is one of the most important habits you can develop. Work at this key point, and your world will change in many positive ways.

Once the credit cards are paid off, never take on credit card debt, again. If this means getting rid of your cards, then get rid of them. If this means limiting how often you use them as you get your life organized, then do it. This is *your* life, take control of it.

It all comes down to priorities. You must know where your money is, what it is earning (or costing you), and whether it could be used more efficiently somewhere else in your life. Stay away from snakes.

You want 21 percent risk free? Pay off your credit cards.

- **Andrew Tobias**

Wise Wanda vs. Careless Kate

Wise Wanda		Careless Kate
Paid Off in Full	<u>$1,388 Credit Card Bill</u>	Paid Minimum
0	<u>Years to Pay It Off</u>	15
$0	<u>Interest paid</u>	$2,525

If Kate had instead invested that $2,525 over a fifteen-year period in a no-load index stock mutual fund earning 9 percent after costs yearly, she would have accumulated (calculation is based on a yearly savings of $168.33 ($2,525 divided by 15 years) a total of:

$5,570.

This example demonstrates different approaches to dealing with a credit card. You can pay it off each month, or you can make minimum payments as you allow the debt to grow larger and larger and larger. Time can be your friend (compound interest on your investments) or your enemy (compound interest on your debt). The choice will be yours.

32

THE ILLUSION

Are you aware of the grand illusion that is going on in our society today? What illusion? I am speaking about the illusion of success, prosperity, and happiness. What do you think you are looking at when you see that new car, big home, designer clothing, and sparkly diamonds? In many cases, you are looking at someone who is leasing property owned by someone else, usually a bank. They look successful, but they're not. They are broke; they just don't want you to know it (and they may not actually know it themselves).

In many societies today, it appears to be more important to some people to project success and prosperity than to actually have it. Presenting the right image and "looking the part" is what counts, right? Wrong. All those material possessions will not bring you success, prosperity, or happiness. I know I am repeating myself, but this is really important so bear with me. Stuff will bring you debt, stress, and possibly bankruptcy and foreclosure. Why would anyone sign up for that?

Let's take a good hard look at this illusion of success and prosperity and figure out why it happens and what you can do about it. Over the last sixty years or so, the environment has made a dramatic shift toward consumerism. This is where you, the consumer, must buy and buy and buy to keep the economy from stalling.

Some very smart marketing folks are coming up with some mighty impressive advertising that will convince you to purchase their products or services. When I say, "convince," I am talking about creating an illusion that you can see yourself in.

The pitch is pretty simple, but don't be fooled; it is also quite brilliant. Pretty/popular/famous people are properly outfitted with amazing stuff, and they look positively incredible and happy. Repeat, and then repeat again, until consumers are able to see themselves in that image. Great marketing campaigns make this happen, at *your* expense.

You see your neighbor loading up on stuff, and your spouse looks at you and says, "Why not us?" This can lead a person or a family to load up on their own stuff. A few payment plans later, and you have all kinds of "neat" stuff. Here is where it gets a little fuzzy.

The neighbors appeared really happy when they got their stuff, but what you find out later is something much different. They were putting on a show. They wanted you to see how happy they were, just like the commercials. What they did not want you to know was how saddled with debt they had become. And while the stuff lost its luster soon after they bought it, the debt and the stress remained behind for years to come.

This brings us to life in the twenty-first century. *The illusion has become the norm.* We find ourselves chasing something that is not real and was never real. *Stop Acting Rich*, by Thomas Stanley, describes how this illusion plays out in homes all over America. Mr. Stanley, who has studied real and not-so-real millionaires for many years, tells us that you can act rich or you can be rich, but you can't do both. Which option will you choose?

You say, "If I had a little more, I should be very satisfied." You make a mistake. If you are not content with what you have, you would not be satisfied if it were doubled.

- **Charles Haddon Spurgeon**

33

CHEAP CLUB FOR SALE!

The technique of bait and switch has been around since people started walking upright. Why do you think that is? It works, that's why. When early man was trying to trade the best club to kill his prey, do you think he advertised the most expensive one to his fellow hunters? Of course not, he picked out the cheapest one made out of the cheapest piece of wood and then advertised it at the cheapest price. Why? So he could entice his gullible brothers in arms into trading with him. Once he got them into his cave, he had them right where he wanted them.

As these future hunters looked at the many clubs for sale, they could not help but be impressed with the best, most expensive club set right beside the cheaper club. It was "cool."

The club owner spent his time playing down the cheap club and playing up the expensive club. He would even cut them a deal because they looked like good hunters, and they needed a break. He was going to "save" them money. They earned it. They deserved it!

The club owner told his customers they could pay for the club over three killing seasons, but they had to buy NOW before supplies ran out. It could be theirs today; just sign on the dotted rock, and go on their merry way.

This technique is used every day to sell you material possessions you do not need. This is called the *bait and switch,* and if you don't prepare yourself for it, you are likely to walk out of the showroom with the "neatest" club that will impress all of the girls and boys. Buyers beware.

While this story is meant to inject a little humor into this serious subject matter, do not underestimate the deadly effects of bait and switch on your life. This technique is used to sell vehicles, furniture, clothing, groceries, electronics, and much, much more. The business advertises a product that appears cheap and almost too good to be true. It is.

The bottom line for any business is getting you through the door, whether that means getting you on the car lot, into the grocery store, on the floors of the department store, or any other place that sells a product or service. Bait and switch is a very effective approach that is used to get you to let go of your money and hand it over to the business.

When you walk in with a picture of the advertisement, the salesperson is there to "help" you with your purchase. He/she sizes you up and figures out what you can afford (think monthly payment). He/she starts the process by downplaying the advertised item and playing up all of the wonderful deals that are now being offered. You are told the sale *will not last*, and you need to buy *now*. Beware! You must learn how to identify this approach and walk away.

They are reaching your emotions to sell you something you most likely do not need. It is important for you to understand the emotional triggers that will cause you to fall for the bait and switch. Beware of Caves!

What is the difference between unethical and ethical advertising? Unethical advertising uses falsehoods to deceive the public; ethical advertising uses truth to deceive the public.

- **Vilhjalmur Stefansson**

34

THAT IS SO "COOL"

Once upon a time, your humble author spent his days trying to be "cool." I wore cool clothes. I drove a cool car. I had cool hair. (Yes, once upon a time I actually had hair that was not pink.) I even spent my days doing cool stuff. Why? I wanted to be liked. I wanted to be popular. I wanted to fit in and be accepted by the people around me. Trying to impress others might make you appear cool, but you will pay a price for this illusion.

Let me paint a picture for you. Heavy debt, lots of stress, broken relationships, closets and garages full of stuff, and a sense of despair that borders on depression are all waiting for the cool people who think they must have the latest-and-greatest thing. Do you like being jerked around by advertising campaigns that show you what the latest cool thing is? Here's an idea. Let's take a look at what was once cool.

Once upon a time, the following items were really cool: leggings, big puffy hair, the mullet, parachute pants, cigarettes, spandex, beanie babies, leisure suits, Members Only jackets, the pet rock, and let's not forget about those beautiful polyester outfits. All of those things were actually cool once upon a time. If you did not have them, then you were some kind of weirdo.

Chasing what is cool is a never-ending process that changes from one moment to the next based on how advertisers steer you toward arbitrary things that are the "new cool." This type of manic behavior works well for the business, not for you.

If you insist on being cool in everything you do and everything you own, you may very well fall down the same deep well of debt into which many people have ended up over the years. Do not allow advertising campaigns to manipulate you on the cool factor. So what is a person to do to stop this from happening?

Stop trying to be cool. I challenge you to be uncool. (Yes, English majors, I realize that uncool is not a word that you will find in the dictionary, but I prefer to think a bit outside the box. I also prefer to make up a word here and there to make my point. From here on out, uncool is officially a word. I have added it to my spell-check dictionary, thank you very much.) Give yourself permission to be uncool; your life will never be the same.

Instead of working so hard on being cool on the outside, I encourage you to be cool on the inside. This will require you to detach yourself from stuff as you develop your self-esteem, self-awareness, and self-respect. Focus on your inner qualities.

Educate yourself on a thing called *the hedonic treadmill.* In a nutshell, human beings tend to adapt to every new and interesting stimulus that comes their way. Here is how it works: When we get that new thing that seems amazing, it is only special for a short period of time. We adapt, and then we seek the next great thing. You need to get off that treadmill!

Feed your soul, not your ego. This process takes you from being materialistic to being a person of quality and substance. This will lay the foundation for your future financial life. Now go out and be uncool!

Be content with what you have; rejoice in the way things are. When you realize there is nothing lacking, the whole world belongs to you.

- **Lao Tzu**

35

I WANT IT NOW!

Instant gratification can ruin you and your financial future. It is very natural to want it NOW, and I would be lying if I told you that I have not been guilty of this kind of thinking at different times in my life. I would also tell you that when I did fall for instant gratification, I paid a very steep price. A price I really could not afford to pay.

It is very easy to fall into this trap of instant gratification. We see the latest technology, the newest car, the newest designer clothing, the exotic vacation, etc. It is very natural to want it NOW, and it is also very costly, especially if we are living the high life based on the amount of credit provided to us from the banking institutions. Buying fun on credit can devastate your financial life.

The question is: How do we stop ourselves from succumbing to these immediate wants? Start with the clear understanding of what is a want and what is a need. Far too many people identify wants as needs. Shelter, food, and water are needs. Most everything else is a want whether we admit it or not.

While there are many ways to deal with this issue, I would first like to identify how you will suffer from the effects of instant gratification. When you must have the newest thing, you will pay top dollar for it and, in many cases, you will go into debt to have it. Of course, when you go into debt, you are actually paying more for that expensive depreciating item due to the interest you will pay on your credit card, car loan, boat loan, etc. This is a mistake you must avoid if you want to see financial freedom in your future.

Why do we allow ourselves to fall for this insidious thing called instant gratification? There are some exceptionally talented folks who put together marketing campaigns that make it mighty tempting to BUY NOW! You have earned it! You deserve it! Nothing down, and no payments for three years! Zero percent loans! And on and on it goes. Everybody and everything seems to be telling you one thing:

Buy now! Pay later!

So what does life look like when you are not playing this game of instant gratification? When they say BUY NOW, you say, *no thanks.* When they tell you that it will CHANGE YOUR LIFE, you say, *I don't think so.* When they promise you that you can have it with NO PAYMENTS AND NO INTEREST, you say, *I think I'll wait until I have the cash to pay for it.* You start to look at life in a totally different and financially efficient way. You have changed, and so has the world in which you live.

You come to realize that those marketing geniuses are simply trying to get you to want something so badly that you are willing to fork over money that you may or may not have. You stand your ground and refuse to play this game that you cannot win.

You start to learn that those brand new items become cheaper and less prone to problems the longer you wait. You will still have the ability to enjoy a few possessions, but they will not own you. You will own them, free and clear.

As we get past our superficial material wants and instant gratification, we connect to a deeper part of ourselves, as well as to others and the universe.

- **Judith Wright**

36

THE NEW HUNK OF METAL

The more new automobiles you buy in your lifetime, the poorer you will become. That is something no car advertisement or bank will ever tell you. It's the truth, but the truth isn't always nice to hear.

Let's face it, most of us like a new car and everything that goes with it. We like the look, the smell, and we definitely like the way it makes us feel. We like to see people stare at our new vehicle and make nice comments. We may strut a little bit, as we feel and look successful. Maybe you just got your first big full-time job. You have earned it. You deserve it. You can afford the monthly payment, no problem. Your ship has come in!

Sorry to burst your bubble, but there is more to this story. You most likely have a new hunk of metal with a big loan attached to it. You have a payment that is due every month, and pretty soon that new car smell will be replaced with some weird odor coming from the back seat. The new car becomes the used car, and you start to wonder why you spent all that money on a new hunk of metal that no longer feels or looks so new. PS You don't actually own that car.

The bank owns the car, you don't. Not so sure? Go ahead and miss a payment, then you will see who actually owns the vehicle. You are using that piece of metal until you pay it off, maybe in three, five, or even seven years. Millions of people live their entire lives always making a car payment. Sometimes they make a car payment, and the car is long gone! There is a better way financially to deal with this issue. It relies on your ability to get in touch with that person in the mirror as you attempt to separate your self-image from your car. Do not let a car or truck define you. Detach your self-image from those vehicles.

When we are young, it sure is enticing to drive the nicest car we can possibly afford just to show everyone how utterly fabulous we truly are, but with age we realize that it was all just a pipe dream. The automobile industry hits us with messages every day on why we need to buy the latest-and-greatest model. They also hit our friends and family with these very convincing messages. Pretty soon everyone believes this wealth-depleting message. It's a lie. It's legal, but it's a lie.

The new car will not make you successful, popular, or happy. That momentary feeling of excitement will be replaced with something not so wonderful. The new hunk of metal will make you poorer than the moment before you signed on the dotted line. That is the real truth.

You must educate yourself on that pesky thing called depreciation. The value of that new car will decline about 5 percent as soon as you leave the lot and approximately 19 percent in the first year. When you drive your new $30,000 vehicle off the lot, you have just lost $1,500. One year later you have lost around $5,700! Would you take nearly $6,000 and flush it down the toilet? That is exactly what is happening when you purchase that new automobile for $30,000.

Most people cannot afford to do this. Buying a quality three- or four-year-old vehicle with cash and driving it until the wheels fall off can be a very wise and financially effective option for many people.

Detach your self-image from your car or truck. Yes, I know I said that already. It is worth repeating. Once you do detach from that hunk of metal, a new vehicle will lose its hold on you. You will be free.

Drive-in banks were established so most of the cars today could see their real owners.

- E. Joseph Cossman

The New Car vs. The Used Car

$30,000 New Car

Starting Value	Depreciation	Year	New Value
$30,000	$5,700 (19%)	1	$24,300
$24,300	$3,600 (12%)	2	$20,700
$20,700	$3,300 (11%)	3	$17,400
$17,400	$2,700 (9%)	4	$14,700
$14,700	$2,700 (9%)	5	$12,000

$30,000 Three-Year-Old Used Car

Starting Value	Depreciation	Year	New Value
$30,000	$2,700 (9%)	1	$27,300
$27,300	$2,700 (9%)	2	$24,600
$24,600	$1,500 (5%)	3	$23,100
$23,100	$1,200 (4%)	4	$21,900
$21,900	$900 (3%)	5	$21,000

37

THE PAYMENT PLAN

Millions of people have been convinced to buy stuff that they cannot afford with money they do not have to impress people they do not know. The monthly payment plan can accomplish this and more!

You do not have to live this way, and you should not live this way if you desire to build wealth over your lifetime. So why do so many people fall into this trap?

Instant gratification certainly plays a role. And let's not forget about advertising and the many salespeople who are there to "help" you with that monthly payment approach as soon as you walk in the door. As I have stated earlier, there are some mighty smart people attempting to help you get what you want now.

Many people go through life gradually increasing their paycheck over time, and as that paycheck increases, so do their monthly payments. The spending goes up as the paycheck goes up. This does not have to be, and it should not apply to you if you want a financially free future. You can live differently than the crowd. You can be free of monthly payments and the debt that goes with them.

Let's take a quick snapshot of how this advertising gimmick works. They get you in the door, and then they convince you to purchase an item for *only* $250 a month. Your mind is quickly realizing that you could have this wonderful car, furniture set, kitchen remodel, whatever, with very little immediate sacrifice. Isn't that wonderful?

No, it is not. That $250 payment is part of an actual debt that you are incurring, and I can assure you it is much greater than $250. You not only take on this large debt, but you also increase it by paying interest on top of what you owe.

This monthly payment mentality will in many cases start multiplying over time very gradually. First, the car payment, then the furniture payment, then the personal loan for the vacation, then the credit card payment, and pretty soon you are broke and trying to figure out how you got yourself into this position. Don't let this happen to you.

You can eliminate your monthly payments. Here is how you do it. Pay cash for anything that depreciates in value. That includes your car, your furniture, your big-boy toys, etc. Getting out of the monthly payment mentality is a big deal. Many people will question why you would do it. You want to be FREE! That's a good enough reason for me, how about you?

The new you can get rid of your debts that have monthly payments, and once that is accomplished, promise yourself that you will never replace those payments and the mentality that goes with them.

The new you may even decide to eliminate that monthly mortgage payment that you have had for years and maybe decades. (This may or may not be wise financially, always consider all options before making this move.) Attack that, and with a little time, patience, and discipline, the mortgage will be gone as well. Take control!

Your present circumstances don't determine where you can go; they merely determine where you start.

- **Nido Qubein**

38

MY JOB STINKS!

My job stinks! There is a good chance that during your working life you will make this statement, sometimes more than once in the same day. Most of us have experienced this feeling. It is not unusual, and you should never feel that you are the only one who is disappointed or let down by what you thought was going to be a great, or even just a good, job. Here is where things can go terribly wrong.

Some individuals live life large outside of their jobs, because they are trying to find the happiness and contentment they do not find within their jobs. This is a mistake that could lead you down a very dangerous path. Let's take a look at two ways you can deal with this very real problem. One way leads to freedom; the other can lead to financial and emotional ruin.

The wrong way to deal with a rotten workplace is to attempt to buy happiness (buy more stuff) with the money you are making from the job. This may result in multiple monthly payments that, in turn, will force you to stay at the very job that you hate. You cannot quit the job because of the debt that you picked up as you were trying to find happiness outside of the job. Of course, you didn't find happiness; you only found out how the rat race really works. Now you are owned by your crummy job and your debt with very few options.

You will never find lasting happiness by simply acquiring more and more stuff. It will actually make you less happy because of the stress of having to work more at a job that you cannot stand just to pay the bills on stuff that lost its value long ago. There is a better way.

The smart and effective way to deal with discontentment at work is to hang in there, work hard, eliminate debt, and save as much money as you possibly can on a consistent basis. Why? Saving is your ticket out of the job that you hate.

Debt will tie you to your job, and savings will provide you the freedom to leave your job. This will give you hope for a better future as you continue to go to work and spend your days doing something that you really can't stand. How long? I don't know, but I can tell you this method works. You must stay with it and avoid getting sidetracked by life and the people you hang out with. We all have friends and maybe family who are trying to buy happiness outside the workplace. Do not let their habits transfer onto you.

Sacrificing today for a better tomorrow will take time. Let's not be naïve. When people tell you to follow your passion (and, yes, I am one of those dreamers), you may not always be able to do it immediately. The key is to identify your passion and then find a path that will get you there.

Saving more of your money and dramatically reducing your spending will put you on the right path. Get on that path, stay on that path, and don't let anyone knock you off that path. Reaching financial freedom is worth the journey. Get on that path.

Your work is going to fill a large part of your life, and the only way to be truly satisfied is to do what you believe is great work. And the only way to do great work is to love what you do. If you haven't found it yet, keep looking. Don't settle. As with all matters of the heart, you'll know when you find it.

- **Steve Jobs**

39

THE AMERICAN DREAM

What does the American Dream mean to you? Do you let others tell you what the American Dream is, or have you made up your own mind? If you drive a new car, have fancy designer clothes, live in a big beautiful house, and constantly buy the latest technology, does that equate to living the American Dream?

Does more and better stuff mean you have achieved the dream of moving from one class of society to a higher class in society? Will that stuff make you rich, successful, and happy?

Millions of people are broke and have little, if any, savings set aside for emergencies. Millions of people have large amounts of debt and plenty of stress to go with that debt. Millions of people are financially illiterate throughout our societies. Do you think there is a connection somewhere between all these issues?

The next time you are out and about, just look around. Many of the people you will see who look successful are not. They are broke or close to it. (Your eyes can deceive you.) Remember, you can look rich, or you can be rich, but rarely can you do both. This brings us to the question I posed earlier to you: Which option will you choose?

If you are ever going to stand apart from this group of people, you must commit to your personal financial education. You can do it, but it won't be easy, nor will it happen overnight. You may be ridiculed, and in some cases you may be shunned. If you're a follower, it will be difficult to stray from the norm. You must be a leader.

Leaders set their own path (remember Jack and Abe). Leaders truly believe in the path they are on, and while they listen to those they respect, they do not stray far from their goals. Their goals drive their thoughts and behaviors. Leaders move forward and do not dwell on the past, nor do they make excuses for their mistakes. They take responsibility and move on. If you are not currently a leader, it is time to become one.

In America we have the opportunity to blaze our own trails. That path should be different for all of us. It is important to live *your* dream. Living someone else's dream will provide you a direct route to unhappiness and resentment. Don't do that, and don't let someone bully you into doing it either.

We can start from humble beginnings and do great things with our lives, but it doesn't just happen. You must make it happen, and that takes some courage, some stubbornness, and a strong belief in yourself. This means taking control of your life and your attitude.

The American Dream does not have to include a whole lot of possessions or money. Chasing after more and more stuff and more and more money is a good way to find misery and bankruptcy.

The American Dream should have a lot to do with freedom. I am talking about the kind of freedom that can provide you with the opportunities to live out your dreams and ultimately find true and meaningful happiness. Choose YOUR American Dream.

Anyone who stops learning is old, whether at twenty or eighty. Anyone who keeps learning stays young. The greatest thing in life is to keep your mind young.

- **Henry Ford**

40

WHERE IS YOUR CREDIT?

Have you checked your credit report lately? Federal law requires that you be afforded access to all three of your credit reports FREE one time every twelve months. You can go to annualcreditreport.com and access all three of your reports (Experian, Equifax, and TransUnion) one time per year at no cost.

Many folks choose to review a different report each quarter throughout the year to stay current with the situation. WARNING: Stay away from the cute commercials with the funny jingles. Those sites cost you money. Avoid them. Now let's get back to those reports.

Many credit reports have missing or outdated information. It is very important to review all of the information carefully to make sure it is correct and current. No one is going to do this for you. You must take control of your credit. So what kind of details on your credit report should you review carefully?

Make sure all of your personal information is correct. If you identify a problem, write it down and continue on. Here is a tip when it comes to bad credit: Anything older than seven years (Chapter 7 bankruptcy is an exception) must be removed. Stay current on these laws; they can change.

Once you have identified all discrepancies, contact the credit bureaus. You can call them and receive clear instructions on how to file a written report that will require them to verify the errors you have found. Take responsibility of the situation; there is a lot at stake. Now let's look at the credit score.

Anytime you take out a loan, the lender will review your credit history and identify your FICO score (Fair Isaac Corporation = credit score). Your score will help in determining whether you qualify for a loan, what interest rate you will get, and how much money the lender will offer you. With that being said, remember this: *Just because a lender offers you money does not mean you should take it.* If you're not sure, wait.

It is important to know how your FICO score is computed. The attachment (under your credit) at thecrazymaninthepinkwig.com will help you further your education on the matter. Here are a few basics:

- Pay your bills on time. Get organized and set them up online by automating the payments.

- Use less than 30 percent of available credit, and strive to keep that number under 10 percent as best you can.

- Do not sign up for new credit cards or drop old credit cards without very good reasons.

Why improve your score? It can save you *thousands* of dollars. When you request a loan, the financial institution will attempt to identify how big a risk you are. The higher your FICO score (get to 760 and your golden), the lower your risk of defaulting on the loan. This translates into lower interest rates (lower cost) for you and less risk to the lending institution. You will have conquered your credit.

If a person gets his attitude toward money straight, it will help straighten out almost every other area of his life.
- **Billy Graham**

41

GET YOUR FOOT IN
THE DOOR?

Many folks who rent a house or an apartment are advised to buy a starter home as a way to get their foot in the door and become a homeowner. Buyers beware. Avoid the starter home.

What is a starter home? A starter home is a home that you purchase even though it is not really all that you want in a home. The idea is that you will buy it, own it a few years, and then sell it and move into the bigger, better home.

Almost everyone—including the real-estate industry, your state and federal government, your family, your friends, and maybe even your children—are encouraging you to buy a home. You hear it everywhere you go, but is it really the best decision for you?

DO NOT buy a home that you cannot see yourself living in for many years. How many? At least five, and you would be wise to live there for a decade or more. Owning a home is expensive. I strongly encourage you to go through the home-buying process as few times as possible in your lifetime. If you're not sure or uneasy, WAIT.

When you purchase a home, whether it is a starter home or the home of your dreams, you are going to spend a lot of money. Besides the down payment, closing costs, property taxes, insurance, and moving costs, you will be spending plenty of money to fit you and your family into the new digs. You are going to spend a great deal of money that you are not going to recoup when you sell.

Keep renting, keep saving, and keep sacrificing until you have enough money for a down payment of 20 percent on a fixed-interest-rate loan that runs fifteen or thirty years. Here is a message few people want you to hear. Get rid of all of your debt BEFORE buying a home.

Yes, this may take some time, and yes, it will delay your ability to purchase that home of your dreams. It will be worth it for the ones who follow this advice and avoid the starter home. Buying a home is a big deal, so prepare, prepare, prepare.

This is not a message you will hear often. Why? Nobody benefits from this message except you. Focus on doing what is best for YOU at this specific time in your life. Governments and corporations are responsible for their decisions (which they don't always handle very well). You are responsible for yours. Do not rush into something as big as buying a home. It could cost you dearly.

Buying a home will be one of the biggest financial decisions you will ever make. Be patient, prepare yourself thoroughly, and take your time as you work your way through this grueling process. There is a great deal of your money at stake. Think it through very carefully before you make the big leap into home ownership.

To be yourself in a world that is constantly trying to make you something else is the greatest accomplishment.

- **Ralph Waldo Emerson**

42

HOME SWEET HOME

What asset has been called the best and possibly only major investment that most people will make in their lifetime? If you answered *your home*, you win the prize. Or do you?

The truth is that your home is not the great investment it is made out to be. At best, it is a poor investment. At worst, it can be a nightmare. Let's take a close look at the numbers BEFORE and AFTER costs. *Far too many people, including myself, have failed to account for the costs incurred when reviewing the investment return on a house.*

Many people over the years have purchased a single-family home with the intention of making a lot of money one day when they sell. But do they? Let's take a look at a home I owned for sixteen years. The purchase price was $127,000, and the house was sold for $210,000. That is a tax-free profit of $83,000! But that was BEFORE costs. I must look at this so-called investment AFTER costs to evaluate just how well I really did. I must subtract the $12,600 that went to the real-estate agent as a commission when I sold the house. That takes me down to $70,400. Well, I still made some money, right? Let's see.

What do you think I was doing during those sixteen years? I was fixing up and maintaining my house, just like most people do. How much did I spend during those sixteen years? It would not be a stretch to say I spent an estimated $12,000 a year paying property taxes, interest on the loan, insurance, and don't forget, I was maintaining and renovating the inside and outside of my home (it was probably more, but I don't want to be to hard on myself). That brings my total costs to $192,000 (16 years x $12,000). That is a loss of $121,600 ($192,000 - $70,400). Ouch!

Owning your own home is not some great investment that is going to make you rich. What about the tax benefits? They benefit the high-income couple that buys the big home. The low- or moderate-income couple who buys the regular size house will have a rather modest benefit. Don't let anyone overhype this deduction. When we consider the property taxes, the insurance, the interest on the loan, the maintenance, and the periodic upgrades, the AFTER cost return makes the personal home a poor investment at best.

Home ownership can be dreadful, bringing with it more stress than you can imagine. Many people can tell horror stories as they explain their home buying and selling experiences. Many times, renting a place is the best way to go at certain stages in your life.

Renting can be the right choice in many situations. It is not money thrown down a gutter. When you rent, you don't pay property taxes, insurance (you might pay for a small renters policy), interest on a loan, or closing costs. You also don't spend money maintaining someone else's place, and you sure don't spend money and time renovating it. Renting provides you the freedom to move at the drop of a hat. When you own a home that can be difficult to do.

Look at a home as a place to raise a family and enjoy a life, not as an investment. Don't buy into the hype of making big bucks on a home. That is the job of the banks and real-estate industry. Instead, focus your efforts on enjoying that place and the people in it. Learn more on the subject from Salman Khan (another wise teacher) by going here: http://www.youtube.com/watch?v=s8GjDRT2MI0.

A home is not a good financial investment and never was. But a home can certainly be a fine investment in your family's happiness…

- **Charles Ellis,** *Winning the Loser's Game*

The Investment?

Purchase price: $127,000

Selling price: $210,000

Profit before Costs: $83,000

Money I paid the realtor when I sold: $12,600

Profit after the realtor: $70,400

Yearly Cost Estimate: $12,000 x 16 years = $192,000

Yearly cost breakdown (will vary with each situation):

Property taxes: [1.5 percent]
Insurance: [.5 percent]
Interest on the loan: [5.0 percent]
Maintenance in and outside the home: [1 percent]
Upgrades on the home: [1 percent]
Other: this includes closing costs, commissions, etc.: [1 percent]

Average yearly cost of owning my home: 10 percent (probably higher)

My average home appreciation: 4 percent (not quite, but close)

My average yearly loss: -6 percent

Net after yearly cost estimate: - $121,600 ($192,000 - $70,400)

Actual tax savings: $1,000 x 16 years = $16,000 (based on a 28 percent marginal tax rate; only incudes savings beyond standard deduction)

Net after tax savings: -$105,600 ($121,600 - $16,000)

Stage IV

LESS SPENDING EQUALS MORE SAVINGS

43

ENOUGH

How many people have you known who said they have enough? I am talking about enough money, enough stuff, just plain *enough*. I would be willing to wager that you can count that number of people on one hand. How close am I?

How much would you need to have enough? Would it be one million dollars? How about six cars, a boat, and a house that looks like a castle? Is that enough? Sadly, there are very high-income people with all kinds of money and stuff who have never reached *enough*.

Whether they are reaching for more money or more stuff, some people just don't get it. Here is the truth: You don't need ten million dollars to have enough, and you don't need the biggest house in the neighborhood to have enough. Enough is a state of mind and a realization of what is really important in life AND what is not so important.

The book *Your Money or Your Life*, by Vicki Robin and Joe Dominquez, goes into great detail explaining this concept of enough and what it can mean to an examined life. Enough means something different to each and every one of us. I encourage you to explore this book and its timeless message. Here is the good news about the concept of enough:

Enough is not a number.

Enough has very little to do with that green stuff that you carry around in your pocket or your purse. Enough is a place you want to reach; a place you can identify as the place to STOP.

We live in a world where we are told more and bigger is better. I have learned that is not true. More is not better. Bigger is not better. As a matter of fact, less is more in many cases. That's right. Less money and less stuff can make your life better, not worse.

Less stuff equals less clutter, and less baggage that you will have to carry around with you in your life. Becoming grateful for what you have will set you down the right path as you reach for something much greater than more stuff. Not sure? I challenge you to read *Your Money or Your Life*; it might cause you to reconsider some of your thinking and what comes from those thoughts.

I am proud to say I have enough, but it wasn't easy nor was it something that happened overnight. I needed help and *Your Money or Your Life* was the book that did it for me. What will it take for you before you have enough? That's a big question and it requires plenty of thought.

This takes an enormous effort on your part and a willingness to learn from others who have come before you. I encourage you to give this concept a try rather than chasing after more and more and more. Here is what I have learned along my journey: Reducing your wants will increase your level of personal fulfillment and ultimately your level of happiness. It did for me and I believe it can do the same for you.

It is the preoccupation with possessions, more than anything else that prevents us from living freely and nobly.

- **Bertrand Russell**

The Fulfillment Curve

What you see below is the fulfillment curve that was made popular by the book, *Your Money or Your Life.* Study the fulfillment curve, reflect on it, and don't ever forget it. Learn to identify when you have enough (nobody is going to show up and tell you). It will set you free in more ways than you can imagine.

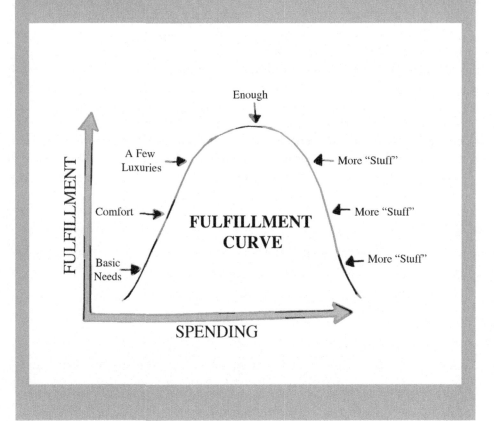

44

THE GAP

The gap can make you wealthy. The gap can make a very big difference in your life. The gap can provide many opportunities in your life. So what is the gap? The gap is the difference between what you make (income after taxes are withheld) and what you spend (all of your monthly expenses and debt payments). That space in between is your savings that you wisely turn into your investments. This is a very important step in creating wealth in your lifetime. Build the gap!

The way to get ahead financially is to widen the gap between your income and your spending as much as you can for as long as you can. This means living well below your means. I am sure many of you reading this are thinking, *well duh, I know that*. Fair enough, so how are you doing with *your* gap?

Far too many people have no gap at all. Let me state the obvious: when you have no gap (living paycheck to paycheck or worse), financial hardship will probably show up somewhere in your near future. Having no gap will cost you dearly.

This must be avoided, and the gap is your ticket out of that trap. The gap can help you achieve financial freedom and reduce the daily stress of life, but it doesn't happen by accident, and it won't happen overnight. It will take a real commitment by you.

The gap will take sacrifice, self-discipline, and patience as you apply the habit of living well below your means over long periods of time. These are attributes you can use to change the course of your financial life. You just have to want it bad enough.

What will happen if you apply the gap over a matter of months and years? *Some will resent you.* You will make them feel uncomfortable because of your self-discipline and courage. *Some will criticize you.* Their version of the good life is surviving paycheck to paycheck and hoping there is enough money at the end of the month to cover all of the stuff they bought at the beginning of the month. Your level of sacrifice will distinguish you from the crowd of stressed-out debtors, and that makes you crazy in their minds. Go figure.

Why should you live the gap when others are not? You want a better life. If you want your life to be different, you must take control of the situation, and that means changing the way you feel, think, and act when it comes to money.

So where do we go from here? Focus on eliminating your debt, especially debt on depreciating assets, and reducing your monthly expenses. Identify what is needed and what is not. Add up your income, and start asking questions.

Are there ways to reduce your spending? Are there ways to reduce your taxes? Are there opportunities to work a side job so you can use that extra money to pay down debt or fund your savings and retirement accounts? Work at answering those questions and always remember: The gap will provide you the freedom to live the life of your dreams.

Winners almost always do what they think is the most productive thing possible at every given moment; losers never do. When you look at what winners and losers actually do moment by moment, the difference between these two divisions of the human race really is that small. But the results of those small differences keep adding to each other at every given moment until they reach a critical size.

- **Tom Hopkins,** *The Official Guide to Success*

45

THIRTY DAYS WILL SET
YOU FREE!

How many times have you purchased something "important" and within a matter of days regretted the decision? There is a solution for this problem. If you commit to it, I promise you will buy fewer items, and what you do buy will mean more to you. It is called the thirty-day waiting period.

Every time you consider purchasing something you want, pause and do not buy it. Give yourself thirty days to think about the purchase, and if you still desire the item, and you can pay for it with available cash in the bank, go ahead and buy it. This type of behavior takes a person who is in control of their emotional state. That can be you. That should be you if managing your money wisely is a top priority in your life.

This rule keeps you from buying on impulse and increases your ability to keep, save, and invest more of your money. It simply requires a commitment from you and a certain degree of self-discipline. Why should you do this? Do you have debt? Is your emergency savings account fully funded? How about your company retirement plan or your Roth IRA?

Spending money on wants BEFORE saving and investing for your future needs is a mistake; a mistake you cannot afford to make. This idea reduces your impulse buys, and that could translate into THOUSANDS of dollars over time.

The thirty-day waiting period can drastically reduce how much money you waste on junk that may or may not bring any real joy into your life. It is your cooling-off period. If you apply this method, you might just be surprised at how many things you do not buy.

The normal marketing plan is designed to get you to buy NOW. The advertisers don't say: *Come on in next month, because this month we are going to screw you with higher prices!* I don't think so. They tell you there is a sale TODAY, and it will only last TODAY. Hurry on down, and *get the deal of the century.* The thirty-day waiting period saves you from falling for this manic, self-defeating behavior.

Let's recap. When you consider purchasing *anything*, take a moment and decide if it is a need or a want. If it is a want (most purchases are wants), do not buy it. Give yourself thirty days to think about the purchase, and if you still desire the item (you will very likely forget about many of your impulse wants), and you have the cash on hand to pay for it, it is yours to buy.

Applying this basic approach can save you a great deal of money over long stretches of time. Take this opportunity to change your buying habits as you take impulse purchases out of your life. Your savings will go up, and your wasteful spending will go down. You will win this war over your emotions and your money.

Every great dream begins with a dreamer. Always remember, you have within you the strength, the patience, and the passion to reach for the stars to change the world.

- Harriet Tubman

46

THE WEAK SPOT

The weak spot is a place in your life where you are weak when it comes to the affection you have for some particular item that borders on excess. That could be your love of cars, eating out with your friends, designer clothing, or maybe your affection for home improvement projects. It could be anything. Here is the problem. People tend to overspend on the things they enjoy.

The weak spot makes you vulnerable, and that could doom any financially free future you hope to have. You must conquer this problem, and that means not letting it control you. Not to worry, I have a very practical and simple approach that can help with this very real problem.

Step 1: Identify what your weak spot(s) are. Not sure? Ask a friend or a loved one. They know. Trust me, they know.

Step 2: Identify how much money you spend per month on that weak spot. This will be easy if you have a spending plan with categories that identify where your money is going. It will be difficult if you do not track your spending. Be honest with yourself, and identify what this number is on a monthly basis.

Step 3: How much money do you have left after you have saved 20 percent of your gross income (more on this in the following chapter) and paid your debts to include your monthly expenses? This is the point where you start budgeting for your weak spot.

Step 4: Budget for your weak spot. Do not go over that budgeted amount in any given month. Let's say you have a weak spot for eating out. After you account for your savings, debt, and expenses, you identify you can afford $220 per month to eat out with your friends and family. That is your number, and you are not allowed to go over that number. If you hit that number in the second week of the month then you are done for the month. Draw that line in the sand, and do not go over it. Do this month after month. This will be relatively easy if you are committed to your financial plan or very difficult if you are not. Ask yourself, how important is financial freedom to you?

Step 5: If you have credit card debt or other high-interest-rate liabilities, you should lock your weak spot up in the closet for the time being. You cannot afford your weak spot when you are living beyond your means.

Only let your weak spot out of the closet when you have the cash to pay for it. If you are using credit to deal with your weak spot, bankruptcy is possibly in your future. Here is a simple strategy that can work for many:

Pay with cash when dealing with your weak spot.

The weak spot is a very dangerous place for any one of us. It is important that we take this issue very seriously. We are all human, and it is natural to have a weak spot or two in our lives. Deal with this issue now before it becomes a bigger issue later. Identify it, budget for it, and control it. There really is no other option worth considering.

If you don't like how things are, change it! You're not a tree.

- **Jim Rohn**

47

THE 20 PERCENT SOLUTION

As early in your life as possible, start saving 20 percent of your gross income each and every paycheck. Pay yourself first automatically at the beginning of each month. This time-tested method works, as you place your money in assets that grow and grow and grow. The amazing thing called compound interest makes this happen. Your job is simply to get that money in the right accounts as you let momentum and time do its thing. Soon, your money will start making money (passive income). This is how wealth is created.

Every time I mention savings, I would like you to replace the word with freedom. That is exactly what savings will bring into your life.

Savings equals freedom.

By saving 20 percent of your income at the beginning of each and every pay period, you will no longer be cemented to your job. Your world will be full of opportunities, because now you will have the ability to change jobs, change careers, and maybe even change the course of your life.

Now I know some of you are rolling your eyes at this notion of saving 20 percent of your gross income (before anything is taken out, including taxes). You have been conditioned throughout your life that you must have stuff to be happy and prosperous. You have received very few messages advocating saving your money. It is natural for you to have become brainwashed into spending your entire paycheck. That is the message you get starting as a young child and taking you into old age (cradle to grave is the marketing term). You may say to yourself, *nobody saves 20 percent*. That would be wrong.

Many people save 20 percent or more of their monthly paycheck. They have made it a priority in their lives and placed it high on their list of goals. They know that saving a nice chunk of their paycheck will allow them to escape the world of work one day.

Now you may make the case that I am trying to brainwash you. Guilty as charged! I am trying to brainwash you into developing habits and behaviors that will change your life in a positive and meaningful way. In many ways, I am trying to undo what has already been done.

Look at your paystub, take 20 percent off the top, and start a savings program. You can divide that 20 percent amount into your emergency savings account, your company retirement plan, and/or your Roth IRA. There will be more on those types of accounts later in the book.

What if you have a lot of debt? You can take 20 percent, above and beyond your monthly bills that you owe on debt, and pay off that debt as fast as possible. When the debt is gone, start saving 20 percent. It will be quite easy at that point.

If you want to achieve wealth, develop their habits, it is that simple. You can learn more about the wealthy and their wealth building habits by reading, *The Millionaire Next Door*, *The Millionaire Mind,* and *Stop Acting Rich* by Thomas Stanley.

The remarkable thing is we have a choice everyday regarding the attitude we will embrace for that day. We cannot change our past... we cannot change the fact that people will act in a certain way. We cannot change the inevitable. The only thing we can do is play on the one string we have, and that is our attitude. I am convinced that life is 10 % what happens to me and 90 % of how I react to it...

- **Chuck Swindoll**

48

AUTOMATIC PILOT

Put your savings and investments on automatic pilot. Some of you are currently employing this strategy as you dollar-cost average your money into your company retirement plan (401(k) for example). This strategy can also be used to start a Roth IRA (covered in a later chapter) or other investments outside of a retirement account.

This approach is not complicated. Based on your plan to save 20 percent, you choose to put $800 per month into your investments (let's say you earn $4,000 per month in gross income). You choose to invest $500 into a stock index fund in your company retirement plan and $300 into a stock index fund in your Roth IRA. When the market is up and your investments are expensive, your money will buy fewer shares. When the market is down and your investments are cheap, your money will buy more shares. Over time you will end up purchasing more cheap shares than expensive shares. This is the value of dollar-cost averaging.

There is no timing the market using this strategy. Timing the market means trying to get in or out of the market based on knowing what direction it is heading. Ignore people who say they can do this. These financial wizards generally get paid to predict the future. That does not make them psychics, and it certainly does not make them correct and wise. Tune them out.

Instead, simply save your money automatically every month and invest it in your appreciating assets, which would include no-load index mutual funds that own stocks, real estate, and bonds. The beauty of this approach is the forced savings over long periods of time.

This method can also be used to invest a big chunk of money that just came into your life (inheritance would be one example). Maybe you have a large amount of money sitting in a bank account. Either way, you may be ready to invest it in stocks or bonds.

History tells us that you would probably be better off to get your money in the market immediately. The US stock market has gone up on a yearly basis, approximately 75 percent of the time. It's okay if the stock market scares you a bit (it scares me a little bit too). You can dollar-cost average the money in over time.

Here is what you can do to reduce your fear. Select a period of months or years over which to dollar-cost average that lump sum into the market. Let's look at an example: You receive a $60,000 inheritance, and you want to invest it in an assortment of no-load index mutual funds. You decide to get that money into your investments over a one-year period. Thus, you will invest $5,000 per month for one year ($5,000 x 12 = $60,000). This only works if you keep your hands off the money that you are setting aside in the bank. Seeing that money as a pot of gold to spend on stuff will sabotage your plan. Be mindful of that.

Dollar-cost averaging is a very effective way to put your wealth creation on automatic pilot, but it takes YOU to initiate it. Dollar-cost averaging has the potential to not only reduce your risk, but also increase your return over long periods of time. Now is the time to implement this basic and time-tested idea. Your future self will be grateful you did.

A man sooner or later discovers that he is the master-gardener of his soul, the director of his life.

- **James Allen**

49

I HAVE A SECRET

I have a secret about how to accumulate wealth in one lifetime. Here it is: Become a great saver as early in life as possible, and invest that money wisely and efficiently over long periods of time while steering clear of most of the financial industry. Sounds pretty simple, don't you think? Here is an example that should illustrate my point.

We have three people who make $2,500 a month (gross income before taxes are withheld). This equals $30,000 per year. Tim saves nothing and spends 10 percent more than he makes. He likes stuff. Beth saves 5 percent of her paycheck while earning a very impressive 10 percent (after costs) on her investments. John saves 20 percent of his paycheck, but instead of investing it, he sticks it in his mattress. Where are they headed?

Tim, the spender, saves nothing and spends 10 percent beyond his means each year. This puts him $3,000 in the hole, plus, he is out the 20 percent in interest paid on the credit card ($600), thus totaling a negative $3,600 for the year. Tim can live this way for a while, but gradually the debt will get bigger, and bankruptcy will have to be discussed in the not too distant future. *Tim is down $3,600 for the year.*

Beth, the great investor, saves 5 percent of her paycheck for the year, which gives her $1,500 ($125 per month x 12), and she earned another $150 (10 percent of $1,500) after costs by investing it wisely in no-load index mutual funds as she avoids all of the "helpers" on Wall Street and beyond. This totals $1,650 ($1,500 + $150). This is good, but Beth's inability to save beyond 5 percent will limit how much her money will grow over time. *Beth is up $1,650 for the year.*

John, the great saver, puts away 20 percent of his paycheck for the year, saving a total of $6,000 ($500 per month x 12), but he earned no interest on that money because it was stuck in his mattress. While a fire or some other calamity could ruin his plan, he is way ahead of the others. *John is up $6,000 for the year.*

The purpose of this example is to highlight the importance of saving your money. Chasing after great investment returns will not benefit you much if you are not able to save a good portion of your paycheck. Of course, the smart move would be a fourth option. Holly just showed up, and she has put it all together.

Holly, the great saver AND great investor, saves 20 percent of her paycheck, just like John, but she does not stick it in her mattress. She will invest her money in those same no-load index mutual funds that Beth selected. Holly earns 10 percent after costs on her $6,000 investment, which gives her another $600, which she will continue to let compound for the foreseeable future. *Holly is up $6,600 for the year.*

Life is full of choices, and each of us will go down a financial path based on the choices we have made. Do you want to be Tim (looks rich but isn't), Beth (poor saver but great investor), John (great saver but poor investor), or Holly (great saver and great investor)?

I think it's pretty clear which person's habits we should emulate. It is critically important to identify the right habits and repeat them over and over again. Follow Holly's example; financial freedom will follow.

The important thing is this: to be able, at any moment, to sacrifice what we are for what we could become.

- **Maharishi Mahesh Yogi**

Life is full of choices

Let's see what happens to our four young people as the years go rolling along (in this example the paycheck stays the same). Everyone's money is compounding (Tim wishes it didn't) except John's, as he has stashed his savings in the mattress. The numbers may surprise you. (The example shows the compounding affect of interest monthly as each year passed.)

Tim	Beth	Years	John	Holly
- $3,600	$1,650	1	$6,000	$6,600
- $61,930	$29,461	10	$60,000	$117,847
- $213,226	$101,598	20	$120,000	$406,394
- $605,648	$288,703	30	$180,000	????????

Tim, the spender, will end up bankrupt. Beth, the great investor, will have a decent amount of money thanks to compound interest, but her limited amount of savings will cost her. John, the great saver, has a nice chunk of money, but inflation has made it worth much less. Holly? After thirty years of diligently saving her money and investing it wisely and efficiently, she has accumulated:

$1,154,812.

50

EMERGENCIES?

We hear it often: you must have an emergency savings account where money is stashed away for a rainy day. Why? Why can't you just tap your credit card or home-equity line of credit when some emergency comes around? Why do you need cash in an account just sitting there?

If you do not have cash set aside for your next emergency, then you will be forced to tap into credit to deal with that problem. This will make your emergency much more expensive AND much more stressful as you pay interest on that money you have borrowed.

Let's say that your furnace gives out, and now you must fork over $2,500 to pay for a new one. Without any savings, you use the credit card, and then you take years to pay it off. That $2,500 problem could easily turn into a $4,000 problem with all of the interest you are going to pay using that credit card.

This is why you need savings stashed away in an easily accessible account that you can reach quickly to deal with your latest emergency.

I know some of you may be thinking: *where is this money going to come from?* Stop spending money on the extras in life and start focusing on being a saver before it's too late. It's not that complicated once you decide to make it a high priority in your life.

As we have already mentioned, human beings who are properly motivated get things done when those things are truly important to them. Saving money needs to become one of your highest priorities. Here are a few guidelines as you move forward toward funding this account.

- Put three to six months of monthly expenses into a savings account. Identify what it takes for you to live on in a given month and then multiply that number by at least three and as high as six. Your tracking spending worksheet will help you here.

- How safe is your job? Put away three months if you have great job security and six months if you have less. When in doubt, go with six months. Jobs are not as safe as we tend to think they are.

- Figure out what it would take for you to sleep well at night. Knowing that money is safely stashed away as you prepare for that next emergency will reduce your fear of not being prepared.

Where do you put it? You will find detailed information on this topic at thecrazymaninthepinkwig.com. Hit on the *savings* tab for a listing of available options. There is no perfect answer regarding where you should place your savings. You must consider all types of risks as well as your particular situation prior to selecting the right type of account.

You may ask whether a person should pay down debt or build up their emergency account. You can't go wrong following Dave Ramsey's first three baby steps that he outlines in his book, *The Total Money Makeover*. Here they are: (1) Put $1,000 aside in savings. (2) Pay down your debt (except your mortgage) as fast as possible starting with the smallest debt and working up to the biggest one. (3) When you rid yourself of the debt, go back and fully fund your emergency account.

The discipline you learn and character you build from setting and achieving a goal can be more valuable than the achievement of the goal itself.

- **Bo Bennett**

51

The Tax Man Cometh

Over your lifetime you will pay a large chunk of money to government agencies in the form of taxes. Let's take a look at just a few: federal income tax, Social Security and Medicare tax (FICA), state income tax, sales tax, property tax, and the gas tax are some taxes that will very likely play a big part in your everyday life. Is that intimidating or what?

The tax code is a mess, and most of it was developed to benefit the wealthy, the powerful, and the well connected. You may not fall in any of those categories, but that should not stop you from using the mess we call tax law to benefit your particular situation.

You can complain about taxes or do something about them. I recommend you do something about them, and that means taking control of your individual situation. This requires a basic level of education on taxes and the self-discipline to act on what is in your best interest.

Here are a few basics: Tax credits reduce your taxes dollar for dollar (great); tax deductions reduce your taxable income (good). There are a limited amount of tax credits, but there are a multitude of tax deductions.

WARNING: Do not buy stuff just for the tax deduction (and be wary of anyone who is pushing a product or service based on this idea). Getting back thirty cents on the dollar is smart only when it was a purchase or an investment that needed to be made.

Now, let's take a close look at a few ways the average person can reduce the amount of taxes (federal and state) they pay on a yearly basis. The goal will be to reduce taxes *without* spending more money.

- Invest in a traditional company retirement plan at your place of employment. This could include a 401(k), 403(b), 457, or a TSP. Every dollar you put away reduces your taxable income.

- Start a business, and own rental real estate. These are two of the last great tax shelters still available to the average person. Educate BEFORE owning.

- Focus on earning passive income. This income is taxed at a much lower rate than earned income. Here are two examples: capital gains and dividends from stocks and bonds. Here is an added bonus; you will pay no FICA tax on passive income.

- Eat out less often, and buy less stuff. You are paying sales tax every time you go out to eat or shop. You are choosing to pay more taxes when you frequent restaurants often and hit the mall for a shopping spree every week.

- Buy a home or a car that is no bigger than you need. A bigger home will require more property taxes. A more expensive car will require a higher tax, as you register that hunk of metal in the first year and for many years to come.

- Take control. Educate yourself on current tax law and employ others (CPA) when needed.

The best years of your life are the ones in which you decide your problems are your own. You do not blame them on your mother, the ecology, or the president. You realize that you control your own destiny.

- **Albert Ellis**

52

THE REPORT CARD

There are some very specific habits that can help a person achieve wealth over time. Here are five habits that can change your life:

(1) Increase your income potential.
(2) Reduce your debt to appreciating assets only.
(3) Increase your savings rate.
(4) Increase your investment returns after costs.
(5) Live far below your means.

What do you say we take a look at how the average person in our society is doing on cultivating these wealth-creating habits? I will provide a grade based on what research tells us on the matter.

Increase your income potential. This is generally done through higher education and hard work. Research shows us that the higher your education level, the higher your future earnings tend to be. Be careful though, higher income does not necessarily mean more wealth. Where most Americans falter is increasing their passive income (your money earning money). There is plenty of work to do on the passive income front. The average person earns a B on this habit.

Reduce your debt to appreciating assets only. Many people do a poor job on this point. Millions of Americans acquire debt on depreciating assets (cars, trucks, big-boy toys, clothing, furniture, etc.). Depreciating assets make you poorer immediately after you buy them (of course, you know that already, right?). The average person has earned a D on this habit.

Increase your savings rate. This is not going well (currently around 3 percent). There are plenty of reasons why, but for whatever reason, the average person tends to save little to nothing from their paycheck. I do believe this has plenty to do with all those advertisements that tell you to buy NOW. The average person has earned another D.

Increase your investment return after costs. The key words here are AFTER COSTS (commissions and ongoing fees). I believe this is the easiest of all of the habits to master. Sadly, the typical person does a poor job. You can thank the financial industry as they take a large chunk of your actual return before they give you what's left (we will try to remedy that later in the book). The average individual has earned their third D.

Live far below your means. Many people live above their means! Look at the amount of credit card debt in America for evidence. Successfully cultivating this habit takes a person who is not easily influenced by advertising or materialism. It takes a leader who wants a better future and is willing to make sacrifices today to reach for something much greater tomorrow. The average individual has earned another D.

Think back to your youth, if you took a report card home to your parents showing a B, and four D's, how do you think they would react? You cannot afford to be average.

You have the ability to get straight A's. It simply takes a commitment from you as you acquire and apply these techniques consistently over time. Make these habits part of your life, and your life will change. I guarantee it.

Character cannot be developed in ease and quiet. Only through experience of trial and suffering can the soul be strengthened, ambition inspired, and success achieved.

- **Helen Keller**

53

ESCAPE

Would you like to escape from the rat race that so many Americans call everyday life? You know, the race where even when you win (top rat), you end up losing. It can be done, and you can do it.

What am I talking about when I use the term escape? I am talking about leaving the world of work as you identify other ways to serve your community and the people you care about. You do this by ridding your life of materialism and the debt and stress that comes with it. Interested?

There may come a time in your life when you have had it with this system we have built in America. You go to a job that brings you little joy only to come home to pay bills on stuff that brings you little in the way of personal fulfillment. Does that sound familiar?

Many people are starting to ask themselves, is this it? Is this what life is all about? No is my answer. There is more to life than trying to be the top rat.

It might just be time to escape and lead a different life, a more fulfilling life. If you have reached that point in your life and you are ready, there is an approach that has worked for many. I have spent plenty of time preparing you for this lesson. I believe you are ready to hear it.

Get rid of all of your debt. This has to be your second step, of course. What is your first step? Honing your mindset. You must believe in your ability to succeed, and you must want to escape the rat race badly enough to make it happen (it will not be easy). You have got to want it desperately.

How? After you have eliminated your debt, build up your savings inside and outside of retirement accounts. Where? Keep reading. I will direct you to the right location and the right investments. By all means, further your education by reading *Your Money or Your Life* by Vicki Robin and Joe Dominguez. They did it. Maybe you would prefer to read *The Simple Dollar* by Trent Hamm. He did it. Here is a wonderful option: *How to Retire Happy, Wild, and Free* by Ernie Zelinski. He did it too.

If you would rather learn about this concept via a blog, you can go to mrmoneymustache.com. He did it before he hit forty! Me? Yes, I did it too. KEY POINT: We all hit the escape button differently. What did we have in common? We developed a plan based on our financial education and then step-by-step we followed through on that plan. This involved developing daily habits that helped us reach our goals. It's possible, and you can do it if you are willing to make the needed sacrifices.

So when you follow this advice, where does it take you? You have no debt and plenty of savings/investments in retirement accounts and nonretirement accounts, all of which are growing gradually over time as they wait for you to start accessing them for your escape needs.

When you reach a point where you're monthly income from your investments is enough to cover your monthly expenses, it might just be your time to hit the escape button. Yes, that sounds like what you think it sounds like. Quit your job and live YOUR life on YOUR terms as you live life following YOUR passions. You have escaped the rat race.

The only freedom which deserves the name is that of pursuing our own good, in our own way, so long as we do not attempt to deprive others of theirs, or impede their efforts to obtain it.

- **John Stuart Mill**

54

DEAR PARENTS

Many times in life, we have heard others say, "If only I knew then what I know now." Well, folks, we can. Not necessarily to help us, but to benefit the generation that will follow us.

If I could go back in time and tell my parents what I know today, what would I say to them? Plenty! Please use this as a reference for that young person in your life, whether a child, a grandchild, or maybe a distant relative or friend. Do not underestimate your ability to guide them toward a better financial future.

Here is what I would say to my parents:

As soon as you find out you are pregnant, start automatically saving/investing in a no-load stock index mutual fund (the total stock market index fund at vanguard.com would work just fine) every month, and place it in your name, not mine.

You could choose to open up a 529 college education plan for me anywhere in the country with as little as $25. The money should go directly to the state to avoid the use of financial salespeople who will do nothing to earn their hefty commissions. You don't need them.

Maybe you would rather invest the money elsewhere so you have more control. You could start investing in a target date retirement fund at a place like vanguard.com. Just be sure to put it in your name. I am a kid, and you should not put money in my name, because when I am eighteen, I might just take off and go to Vegas with that drama queen you hate!

Keep putting money into this fund every month, and add to it as often as possible around my birthday and the holidays. When I graduate from high school and head off to college or the world of work, put limitations on that money and how it is distributed. Give it to me in increments gradually over time. DO NOT give it to me in one big lump sum. I will just blow it.

Keep the presents to a minimum. I will be just as happy with two or three presents rather than twelve or thirteen on my birthday or the holidays. If you keep showering me with those material possessions, you are going to make me think that is how one demonstrates love. Smother me with your time and affection; that's all I really need. Send those gifts to my investment account, and while you're at it, ask all of the other adults in the family to do the same.

Teach me by example. I am going to pick up your habits. Show me how you save for a rainy day. Show me how to save for retirement. Show me how to live a good, decent, balanced life that includes frugality and limited waste while cherishing the people in my life. *I am going to ignore your words much of the time, but I will always be watching you.*

Teach me about money management. I am counting on you to prepare me for the world of money. Don't worry when I roll my eyes at you and act like I don't care. Let's face it, I am a kid, and it's not cool to listen to your parents. Bribe me, fine me, play games, do whatever is necessary, but do it. Okay, Mom and Dad, it's all in your hands now. I am just a kid who is going to be born with absolutely no knowledge about money. Please, help me.

You can never really live anyone else's life, not even your child's. The influence you exert is through your own life, and what you've become yourself.
- **Eleanor Roosevelt**

Stage V

BECOME THE WISE INVESTOR

55

THE FOX AND THE HEN HOUSE

Who do you trust when it comes to receiving an education about money? It makes sense to contact and request help from the people who work in the financial industry, right? I am sorry to tell you, that is not a good idea. Why? No matter how well educated a person is, if they have a conflict of interest or some personal stake in the information they are providing, you must stay skeptical with the material they are sharing with you. Would you trust a fox that loves chickens and the eggs they hatch, to guard a hen house?

The financial industry compensates their salespeople (investment brokers, financial advisors, life insurance agents, etc.) primarily using commissions given based on the different products they peddle. Yes, peddle. These experts are generally encouraged to promote the products and services that benefit their firm the most. This is also where self-interest kicks in. Those salespeople will be selling products that benefit them the most. You are looking at salespeople dressed up in pretty outfits trying to figure out how to reach your pocketbook.

You might be surprised to learn that many people in the financial industry spend more time learning how to sell than improving their level of financial knowledge. Why is that? The financial expert benefits monetarily much more by becoming a great salesperson rather than a great financial teacher.

If you could make $200,000 a year becoming a great salesperson or make $50,000 a year becoming a great financial educator, which option would you select? I think you and I both know how most people would answer that question. So how can we protect ourselves?

Stay far away from financial salespeople. This also includes the firms they work for, which may include: Edward Jones, Morgan Stanley Smith Barney, Goldman Sachs, Merrill Lynch, and UBS Wealth Management to name a few. Lehman Brothers and Bear Stearns used to be on that list, but the fat cats and their big bonuses went bankrupt, so that's two fewer financial firms you have to worry about.

Who should you listen to when it comes to investing? Here are a few people I recommend: John Bogle, Charles Ellis, William Bernstein, Burton Malkiel, David Swenson, Daniel Solin, and Warren Buffett.

Nobody cares more about protecting your money than you. This is why you must identify the people you can trust. Find those teachers, learn from them, and then take action based on what is best for you going forward. This advice goes for the individual investor as well as the large institutional investors. This list would certainly include charities, large endowments, and pension funds. (Yes, you should ask how your institutions are investing YOUR money.) The message is pretty clear. Stay away from the fox (commissioned salespeople).

Stop trying to find the right fox to guard your hen house. Stop trying to retrain the fox to guard your hen house. You don't need the fox, you should not trust the fox, and you definitely cannot afford the fox. (He is stealing your eggs that you will need in the future.) It is time for the hens (you, me, and those big institutional investors) to take charge of our own hen house. Kick the fox out and guard your own hen house!

You don't need 99.9 percent of what Wall Street is selling. It's expensive, unsuitable, or stupid. Most investments are designed to profit the brokers, banks, and insurance companies, not you. They should carry a warning label: "Beware! This financial product may be injurious to your wealth!"

- **Jane Bryant Quinn**

56

THE EFFICIENT INVESTOR

The argument between investing in index stock mutual funds versus managed stock mutual funds (this of course takes place after a person sees the futility of investing with individual stocks) has been going on for quite some time. John Bogle, creator of the first publicly offered index fund, has pushed and prodded individual and institutional investors to make this type of investment their core investment, even though many people in the financial industry stated that he was "crazy" to promote such a thing.

Since the mid-1970s, there have been dozens of passively managed index mutual funds created to mimic all types of indexes. The question is whether they will provide you a higher return on your investment after costs than managed mutual funds run by smart people in the field of personal finance and investing.

To answer this question, let's first identify what these things are. Managed stock mutual funds are investments that are run by smart people. These well-educated and capable managers are trying to out-pick and outsmart other experts on Wall Street. This is where the majority of individual investors place their money, as they are attempting to *pick the winning horse*. This is called, "reaching for *alpha*."

Do not try to gain an advantage in the market by picking the right manager at the right time. It has not worked consistently in the past, it is not working in the present, and it is very unlikely to work in the future. You should not attempt to play this loser's game. Stop chasing alpha, and don't chase past performance; it's that simple. Select no-load index mutual funds with ultra low expense ratios (this is how the investment company makes the majority of their money).

An index mutual fund simply takes pooled investments (money invested individually by many people) and mimics an index such as the S&P 500 or the Wilshire 5000. Index funds are where institutions and individual investors should be investing their money. These funds are boring and cheap, but are they really the best investment option?

Yes, investing in index mutual funds trumps managed mutual funds and individual stocks by a wide margin. They win because of their low expenses (no commissions and small expense ratio), low turnover (less buying and selling), tax efficiency (fewer capital gains due to reduced selling), and their simple approach to owning the market. The research is in, and it keeps telling us the same thing. Own no-load index mutual funds.

I am a reformed "smart" investor. In the past, I thought I could pick the right managed mutual funds with the right managers who could beat the market. I was wrong.

Over the years, I have moved out of managed mutual funds and into index mutual funds. I currently own only no-load index mutual funds. I recommend you do the same. Another option is to own target date retirement funds that contain index funds. One fund can do it all, and that may work for many people. More on those funds later in the book.

You should also know about *survivorship bias*. Hundreds of managed mutual funds have died a slow death, and their poor performance numbers were buried with them. If the deceased mutual fund headstones were counted (they rarely are), investing in an index fund would make even more sense. Be the efficient investor. Buy no-load index mutual funds.

Most investors, both institutional and individual, will find the best way to own common stocks is through an index fund that charges minimal fees. Those following this path are sure to beat the net results (after fees and expenses) delivered by the great majority of investment professionals.

- **Warren Buffett**

Recommended Mutual Funds

Go to vanguard.com to learn more.

Stock Index Funds	Expense Ratio
Total Stock Market Index Fund	.05%
500 Index Fund	.05%
Total International Stock Index Fund	.16%
REIT Index Fund	.10%
Small-Cap Value Index Fund	.10%
Small-Cap Index Fund	.10%
Value Index Fund	.10%

Bond Index Funds	Expense Ratio
Total Bond Market Index Fund	.10%
Short-Term Bond Index Fund	.10%

Target Date Retirement Funds	Expense Ratio
Target Retirement 2010-2060	.16% − .18%

57

THAT IS A LOAD OF S*&#!

There are over 5,000 mutual funds in the United States. The majority of these funds contain no load (commission). Yet, the majority of people invest in mutual funds that charge a load. Why would a person pay a commission to invest their money when they don't have to? Does the commission improve their return on investment? No. Empirical data retrieved from multiple research studies shows us that load funds perform no better than no-load funds, and when you factor in the brokers' commissions, they lose consistently over time. So why do people do it? Financial "experts" overly influence millions of people.

Let's take a look at an analogy that may explain this point in a better way. Would you rather buy a gallon of milk (mutual fund) at your local grocery store (a no-load family like Vanguard), or pay a guy in a suit (a broker, life insurance agent, or financial advisor) to buy the same gallon of milk, paying him a 5.75 percent commission? This guy tells you he is a milk expert, but let's be honest; he is no more qualified than you in selecting the right gallon of milk. All you have to do is find the grocery store on a map and take your happy self down there to buy your own gallon of milk.

Paying the milk guy a commission is a waste of your money. The same can be said for paying an advisor or broker to purchase a mutual fund. That load is going to the salesperson, not to the mutual fund. The milk will not taste any better just because you paid a guy to pick it up (he will also end up buying more expensive milk as he "helps" you). This is a message the financial industry does not want you to hear. Why? They don't want you to know that they are not needed.

It is absolutely crazy that so many people in America and abroad make this critical mistake. Your fellow citizens are going down to the local grocery store and paying some person in a lovely outfit to pick up an expensive gallon of milk.

The financial industry wants you to believe they are the experts in buying the right gallon of milk, at the right price, at the right time. They are not, and the sooner you learn that in your investing life, the better off you will be, as you will keep more of YOUR money.

Start educating yourself on the investing world and specifically how to invest wisely while reducing your costs on a yearly basis. There is plenty of available information on investing at my website and contained in some of the wonderful books listed in the appendix of this book.

The teachers are waiting to provide you with the answers you will need to become a wise and efficient investor. Use them, and remember, when you go to the store: Buy your own gallon of milk!

Even as Wall Street belittles your investment abilities, it also wants you to believe you can beat the stock-market averages. This, of course, is contradictory. But it is also entirely self-serving. The more you trade and the more you invest with active money managers, the more money the Street makes. Increasingly, some of the market's savviest investors have turned their back on this claptrap. They have given up on active managers who pursue market-beating returns and instead have bought market-tracking index funds. But Wall Street doesn't want you to buy index funds, because they aren't a particularly profitable product for the Street. Instead, Wall Street wants you to keep shooting for market-beating returns. That is why you should be suspicious when you hear talk of the supposed "stock picker's market."

*- **Jonathan Clements**, You've Lost It, Now What?*

Managed Funds vs. Index Funds

The numbers stated below were taken from the mutual-fund tracking agency, Morningstar. These numbers reflect how many smart money managers failed to beat their respective indexes over a fifteen-year period spanning from 1997 to 2011.

These numbers do not reflect loads (commissions) paid to salespeople or the dead mutual funds (funds that were closed due to poor performance) that no longer exist. The failure rate would be higher if they did.

Percent of managers who failed to beat their index

Large-Cap Stock Mutual Funds: **84%**

Mid-Cap Stock Mutual Funds: **96%**

Small-Cap Stock Mutual Funds: **95%**

International Stock Mutual Funds: **64%**

Short-Term Bond Mutual Funds: **98%**

Intermediate-Term Bond Mutual Funds: **87%**

58

DIVIDE AND CONQUER

In the world of investments, asset allocation belongs right up there at the very top of the list when attempting to calculate the expected returns on our money. It is critical that we learn how to divide up our assets and conquer the markets as we diversify over many industries and many countries. So what is asset allocation?

Asset allocation is usually discussed in the context of the allocation of your investments between stocks, bonds, and cash. Bonds and cash will serve as one allocation, and stocks will serve as another. *Asset allocation has more to do with the actual return on investment than any other variable.* What doesn't play a big part? Timing the market or picking the right stocks and bonds are two approaches you should avoid. You don't have to be the smartest person on Wall Street, and you shouldn't try to be.

When I say an asset allocation of 80/20, I am referring to having 80 percent of your assets in stocks and 20 percent of your assets in bonds and cash. Identifying the proper asset allocation needs to be one of the first things you identify when you are ready to start investing your money.

The asset allocation you select, whether that is an 80/20 split or maybe a 50/50 split, is designed to fit your goals, time horizon, tax situation and risk tolerance. This involves the use of modern portfolio theory as we attempt to view our investments as a whole, rather than individually.

What is the proper asset allocation for you? That is a simple question with no simple answer. It depends based on how you answer those issues like risk tolerance, time horizon, goals, and your precise tax rate that deals with your marginal and effective tax rates.

There are many ways to deal with this dilemma, and there is no perfect solution. Here is a rule of thumb that will work for some people: John Bogle (a very wise teacher) recommends that we simply take our age and allocate our bonds and cash to that amount.

Here is one example: If you were forty years old, you would assign 60 percent of your portfolio toward stocks and put the other 40 percent in bonds and cash. Mr. Bogle would admit this is a conservative approach, but he would also tell you that most people are not as risk tolerant as they say they are, which causes them to freak out and sell when the market tanks, and IT WILL tank at different points throughout your life.

There is no perfect asset allocation, and that means you must get to know your particular situation very well. Take your time and figure out what is right for you. Any book written by William Bernstein (another great teacher) will help you further your education on this important issue.

Now what? Continue to educate yourself on the asset allocation concept, develop a plan that fits your needs (what are you investing for), identify the low cost way to do it (no-load index mutual funds or target date retirement funds that own index funds), execute your plan (keep it simple and buy your funds at vanguard.com when possible), follow and update your plan (rebalance every year or so as needed), and finally, stay the course (hold those funds for decades).

No matter how you allocate your assets, you will always wish that you had assigned more to the best performer and nothing at all to the worst performer. Since no one can predict which these will be, the safest course is to own them all, and thereby, as best you can, assure yourself of not being devastated by an Enron or a Lehman. When you minimize your expenses and diversify, you forego bragging rights with the neighbors and in-laws, but you will also minimize the chances of impoverishing yourself and the ones you love.

- **William Bernstein**, *The Investor's Manifesto*

Asset Allocation by the Numbers

    These numbers were retrieved from vanguard.com and deal with the historical returns based on a portfolio divided up between stocks and bonds. The time period runs from 1926 to 2012. Note: This time period includes the great depression and the lousy stock returns of the first decade of this century. Use these historical averages as a guide when you are identifying the right asset allocation for you.

Asset Allocation Options	Historic Average
100% Bonds	5.5%
80% Bonds / 20% Stocks	6.7%
70% Bonds / 30% Stocks	7.3%
60% Bonds / 40% Stocks	7.8%
50% Bonds / 50% Stocks	8.3%
40% Bonds / 60% Stocks	8.7%
30% Bonds / 70% Stocks	9.1%
20% Bonds / 80% Stocks	9.4%
100% Stocks	10.0%

59

HOW MUCH CAN YOU HANDLE?

Most of the time when folks in the financial industry speak about risk, they are referring to the market risk of a particular investment over a short period of time. What is rarely discussed is the long-term risk of your investments. The long-term risk must be addressed if you are going to build wealth over time.

When you put some of your income aside to purchase bonds, stocks, real estate, or maybe income-producing land, you are taking a risk of losing some of your capital. That is your short-term risk, and that is what you generally hear about from the many financial pundits when discussing this issue. Why? Nobody wants to lose money.

When a person loses money, they feel sick to their stomach, dumb, and scared. The simple truth is this: If you want higher returns on your money, you must take on more short-term risk. There is no getting around this uncomfortable issue.

The best investors are able to push aside short-term risk for long-term gain by calculating their risk and the possible reward. Here is an example of what not to do: You shun stocks and real estate and instead choose to keep your money in the bank and earn .2 percent with almost no risk of loss of capital.

This takes care of your short-term risk (your money does not go down in value), but your long-term risk is high due to current and future inflation (your money is shrinking year after year after year). That is a big deal, and you must address this very important issue as you evaluate your investments over different periods of time.

So what is a person to do? Look at the historical returns on each type of investment you are considering. Stocks have historically provided the best return on your money (in any given year any traded asset can go down). The numbers stated below are nominal returns averaged out over a very long period of time before inflation and before costs. They may or may not reflect future returns. Know your history!

- Stocks: 10%

- Real estate: 8% (income producing Real estate including REITs)

- Bonds: 5%

- Cash: 3%

If you want higher returns, you must allocate more of your money toward higher-risk investments. You can learn more on this subject by reading William Bernstein's wonderful book, *The Four Pillars of Investing* or Burton Malkiel's classic, *A Random Walk Down Wall Street*. Both of these books will enlighten you on this very important topic. Now go out there and take some risk!

Should individual investors have reason to abandon the stock market because of the increased volatility rapid-fire trading can cause? Not at all. Investors saving for retirement have no reason to fear day-to-day or week-to-week volatility. The correct response is not to "do something" but rather to "just stand there."

- **Burton Malkiel**

60

THE FREEDOM PLAN

There are many types of retirement plans in America. I call them freedom plans because one day they will provide you the freedom to leave the world of work. These plans are offered by many entities, including city, state, and federal government agencies, as well as private corporations and even nonprofit organizations. They can come in the form of a pension or defined contribution plans, such as a 401(k), 403(b), 457, or TSP. An individual 401(k) or SEP would apply to small business owners. You might select the Roth versions (money invested after it has been taxed) or the traditional plans (before it is taxed).

If you are lucky enough to have a pension (a defined benefit plan funded by your employer and not you), then count your blessings. Millions of people will not see a pension in their lifetimes. This means they must contribute to their own freedom plan on a consistent basis if they want a financially free future.

The immediate benefit of a traditional retirement account like a 401(k) is a deferral in your federal and state income taxes (if you have a state income tax). This is done when you have money taken out of your pay before taxes are withheld, thereby reducing your taxable income.

If you invest $10,000 each year, you have effectively deferred $3,000 worth of taxable income from your federal and state income taxes, based on a 30 percent federal and state marginal tax rate. You are reducing your current taxes AND saving for your retirement. Another benefit may involve your employer matching a percentage of your contributions. This is free money! Go get it.

Many times that free money is provided in company stock. Do not keep more than 5 percent of your 401(k) invested in your company stock. Why? You will be taking great risk with owning stock in only one company. Putting all your eggs in one basket is a BIG mistake. It's not worth the risk.

So how much do you invest? I hope the first number that popped in your head was 20 percent. If you earn $60,000 a year as a family, which is $5,000 a month, then you would simply put away $1,000 a month (20 percent of $5,000) and do that month after month after month.

Do not cash out your freedom account (if you do, you will pay taxes and penalties). Do not borrow from your freedom account (you'll be stealing from your future). Finally, avoid listening to Bill in the break room. He isn't the financial wizard he thinks he is.

So what funds do you select in your freedom account? If broadly diversified stock index funds are offered, focus on them. If not, look toward a target date retirement fund that holds index funds. If neither of these types of funds is offered, you need to ask your company why that is. Every retirement plan should offer at least one broadly diversified index mutual fund. Demand it!

In most cases, your money will initially go into a very safe fund. Do not keep it there. As soon as possible, have your contributions go to a broadly diversified index stock fund(s) or a target date retirement fund that corresponds to the year in which you plan to retire. Start today!

Give yourself all the time you can. Begin to invest in your 20s, even if it's only a small amount, and never stop. Even modest investments in tough times will help you sustain the pace and will become a habit. Compound interest is a miracle.

- **John Bogle**, *Common Sense on Mutual Funds*

61

PUT YOUR MONEY IN THE SAFE

A Roth IRA is kind of like a safe that protects what you place in it. The Roth IRA provides tax-deferred earnings (you don't pay taxes on the accumulated earnings during the year) and tax-free money (you will never pay tax on your earnings). These are great benefits, but they come with rules and regulations.

You cannot take out your earnings before you are 59.5 years old without paying a 10 percent penalty on that money (though there are exceptions). However, you can pull the principal out (the money you put in) at any time and for any reason without paying a penalty or taxes.

So what exactly is a Roth IRA? Imagine a large safe (Roth IRA) into which you decide to put your investments. You have a no-load index mutual fund that you want to invest in, but you want to make it a Roth IRA. Instead of investing in the fund as a taxable investment outside of retirement, you place it in your safe. Now that fund is your Roth IRA.

You can find that safe at many types of institutions. There are banks, credit unions, brokerage houses, and a litany of investment firms. I would recommend you start and end your search at vanguard.com.

Vanguard is the largest investment management company in America. They also provide investing options for many people outside the shores of the United States. Take some time to learn about this wonderful company and the services they provide. They have served me well for over twenty years. I believe they can do the same for you. (I have absolutely no affiliation with Vanguard.)

What type of investments should you place in your Roth IRA? No-load index mutual funds and/or target date retirement funds of course. KEY POINT: You must earn income (from a job) to fund a Roth IRA (the exception to this rule is a spousal IRA that is funded by the working spouse for the spouse who is not working). If you place $5,000 in a Roth IRA, you must have earned at least $5,000. What you do after opening the account is very simple. You just keep feeding the account each and every month (dollar-cost averaging) as you keep your costs ultralow.

There are income limits, contribution limits, and many other rules that govern a Roth IRA. Take the time to understand the current guidelines before investing your money. As always, educate yourself, and then take action based on what is best for you.

There are also many kinds of IRA's that are not Roth IRAs; safes that are named "traditional" and "simple," to name just two. The reason you do not hear much about the others is because the Roth IRA is a much better deal for most people. You can learn more on this issue by going here: https://investor.vanguard.com/what-we-offer/iras/traditional-iras-and-roth-iras.

A Roth IRA can be designed to help you reach many financial goals. It can be used for a college education. It can be used for a down payment on a first-time home purchase. It can even be used as a secondary emergency account. Here is the bottom line: The Roth IRA can serve you in many ways beyond just retirement. Educate yourself, get started, and stay with it. Your financial future is what YOU make it.

The most efficient way to diversify a stock portfolio is with a low-fee index fund.

- **Paul Samuelson,** Winner of the 1970 Nobel Prize in Economics

62

TULIP ANYONE?

Do you know your financial history? Let's take a look. Could a mere tulip bulb be worth $50,000? It is if someone is willing to pay the price! It may sound preposterous, but this is exactly what happened in Holland in the 1630s.

The first tulip bulb was imported into Holland around this time. Gradually, tulip bulbs became a status symbol for the wealthy. Eventually, these plants became a hot-ticket item in neighboring Germany, as well. Here is where it gets interesting. A few tulip bulbs contracted a plant virus called mosaic. This caused the tulip petals to bloom with beautiful flames of amazing color. *This would change lives.*

Initially, only the true tulip lovers bought tulip bulbs, but it quickly attracted speculators looking to make a quick profit. It did not take long before the tulip bulbs were traded on local market exchanges, which were very similar to today's stock exchanges.

By 1634, tulip mania had spread to the Dutch middle class. Soon, it would spread throughout the rest of Europe. *The mania had taken hold.* Tulips were making people rich!

The name of the game was to buy low and sell high. The whole Dutch nation was caught up in a sweeping craze as many people traded in everything they owned just to acquire one tulip bulb. Sadly, as all bubbles do, the tulip craze burst, and then things got ugly. There always comes a point when the crowd says, *that's too much.* The price dropped and kept dropping. When nobody is willing to buy, prices plummet. Thousands of people were ruined and lost everything. 5

So why do I tell this very sad story? During our lifetimes we will experience many crazy, preposterous manias similar to the tulip craze. Does anyone remember the technology craze in the 1990s? What about the recent housing bubble that devastated so many families?

During a craze, people say it is normal, that the world has changed. They are wrong. It is important that you understand a craze when you see it. Don't be greedy, and that means don't be a speculator. Speculators who get exaggerated returns should not be surprised when the tipping point comes and there are no buyers. When the bubble pops, it gets ugly.

If someone tried to sell you a tulip for $50,000 today, you would call him mad. Once upon a time, that was a deal! In recent times, there were people who thought they were getting a steal with their home purchase. They bought that $50,000 tulip bulb.

You must become educated on the history of investing if you hope to avoid making big mistakes with your money. It is wise to identify good investments, but it may actually be more important to know what the bad ones look like.

Here are a few investments you should avoid: artwork, gold, silver, timeshares, undeveloped land, individual stocks, private equity (including private REIT's), cash-value life insurance, annuities (with the exception of the immediate fixed annuity), collectibles, and anything that remotely deals with gambling (the lottery for example). The wise investor avoids speculation and embraces the idea of long-term investing with those boring and efficient no-load index mutual funds. Be the wise investor.

Don't get confused about stockbrokers and mutual fund salespeople. They are usually very nice people, but their job is not to make money for you. Their job is to make money from you…

- **Charles Ellis**, *Winning the Loser's Game*

63

CORRUPTION

I hope most of you know what Enron was and what some Enron officials did once upon a time. If not, here is another quick history lesson. Enron was a small energy company based in Houston, Texas, in the 1990s. They quickly grew (at least on paper) to become the largest energy company in the United States.

This up-and-coming business controlled energy markets across the country in ways that no company had ever done before. Life was grand, and the bonuses were big. Then the house of cards started to collapse.

We found out later that Enron was run by corrupt men who were willing to "cook the books." One book was allotted for the IRS, and the other truthful book was known only to the corrupt few in and around the boardroom.

Next came the inevitable: the company collapsed, and the crooks went to jail or killed themselves one by one. Suffice to say, *no one lived happily ever after*. So why am I telling you this wretched story? Thousands of individual workers for Enron lost their jobs in one fell swoop, and many of them had made one of the worst financial decisions of their lives.

When you work for a company and receive matching funds in your 401(k), much of the time those matching funds come in company stock, Enron stock in this example. So far so good, right? You are working hard and doing your job, and life seems to be peaches and cream as your matching Enron stock (which is free by the way) is going up, up, and away. Here is where it gets ugly.

Many Enron employees went into their 401(k) accounts and transferred their diversified mutual funds into Enron stock. They put all of their eggs into one basket, the Enron basket. They listened to their buddies in the break room. They listened to the corrupt bosses in the boardroom. They were going to be rich! Here was the problem: They were no longer invested in thousands of different companies in the United States and overseas. These employees were invested in one company—Enron—and that was a terrible mistake.

When the news of corruption hit, Enron stock plummeted, and all those employees were scrambling to get out, but it was too late. They not only lost their jobs when their company was run into the ground by the crooks; they also lost their retirement savings when their Enron stock lost all its value. Thousands of employees walked out of their offices that day with no job AND no retirement savings.

If you receive matching stock from your employer, keep it to a minimum amount. How? When it is allowed, sell those individual stock shares and transfer the proceeds into diversified mutual funds (preferably index mutual funds) within your 401(k). This will dramatically reduce your market risk as you spread your money over the entire world.

NEVER put all of your retirement savings into one stock, no matter how good the company is, no matter how well the stock has done, and no matter what Bill says in the break room or the big shots say in the boardroom. Do not forget Enron.

Anyway, no drug, not even alcohol, causes the fundamental ills of society. If we're looking for the source of our troubles, we shouldn't test people for drugs, we should test them for stupidity, ignorance, greed and love of power.

- **P.J. O'Rourke**

64

FINANCIAL PORNOGRAPHY

How many people do you see in the investment world telling you how to make money? How many individuals are telling you how they can make you rich in stocks, real estate, or maybe gold? How do you know who is honest, who is ignorant, and who is a just a good old-fashioned crook? It's not always easy, but there are certainly some guidelines you can follow to help you avoid being "taken."

If it is an infomercial, TURN IT OFF! If they are telling you what stock to buy, TURN IT OFF! If they have found some "secret" way to profit in the stock/bond/gold/silver market, TURN IT OFF! If they are guaranteeing high returns with little risk, TURN IT OFF!

Do not make financial decisions based on what you see or hear coming from the boob tube. Please reread that last statement again and never forget it. There are a lot of people chasing after your money.

The infomercials and financial pundits are simply trying to sell you on their ability to outguess the stock market and its many investors. They don't have to be right, and most of the time, they aren't. Don't fall for their pitch, no matter how good it may sound. They cannot pick the winners consistently and they cannot predict the future. You should ignore their rambling commentary.

So what is a person to do if they are not supposed to listen to the suits and the pretty outfits with all those wonderful credentials after their name? *Go to the teachers.* When you are ready for a financial education, go to the people who will educate and not sell.

One of the most important things the average person can do with personal finance is learning how to identify the right people to learn from while avoiding the wrong people. Again, select the teachers, not the salespeople. This continues to be one of the major themes of this book.

There are thousands upon thousands of hucksters who are trying to make money off the average person's financial ignorance (the crooks and the not so ethical financial helpers belong in this group). They are selling you dreams and feeding your greed and fear. There are even self-proclaimed experts who make fools of themselves on television with bells and whistles and exaggerated claims that are more hype than reality. Do not let your guard down. There will always be somebody around the next corner peddling the next great thing. Run away from these people.

Jane Bryant Quinn, author of *Making the Most of Your Money* and *Smart and Simple Financial Strategies for Busy People,* is famous for coining the term "financial pornography." It may be hard to explain, but you know it when you see it.

Miss Quinn was right then, and she is still spot-on today. Tune the salespeople out, find your teachers, and absorb as much financial information from them as you possibly can.

There are two kinds of investors, be they large or small: Those who don't know where the market is headed, and those who don't know that they don't know. Then again, there is a third type of investor, the investment professional who indeed knows that he or she doesn't know, but whose livelihood depends upon appearing to know.

- **William Bernstein,** *The Intelligent Asset Allocator*

65

HOW DO YOU DEAL
WITH STORMS?

I hope you lose $100,000 in the stock market at some point in your life. Yes, you read that correctly, and no, I have not lost my mind (well, maybe a little). Let's take a look back just a few years. In 2008, I lost about $180,000 in the stock market. In 2009, I made approximately $120,000 in the stock market. So what happened? Was I an idiot in 2008 and then a genius in 2009? The answer is no on both counts.

If you invest in the stock market, which includes stock mutual funds, you will lose money in some years. I guarantee it. Many times over the years, I have counseled people on investing their money. I look them straight in the eye and tell them, "Some years you will lose money."

To this they invariably say, "Okay." Then 2008 comes along, and those same people FREAK OUT. They call me up to ask what is going on with the crazy market. I remind them of our conversation, and they reply, "I didn't think it would be this bad!"

If you invest in stocks, you MUST be ready and willing to ride out the storms. There will be storms! Did I enjoy losing all that money in 2008? No, I wish it had not occurred. I also wish for world peace, but that's not going so well either, now is it? So what did I do? I stayed the course.

I continued to invest automatically into the stock market during 2008 and 2009, whether it was going up or down. I did not try to time the market. I am an investor, not a speculator. There is a clear distinction. If you want to build wealth over time, be an investor.

Investing in stocks is not for the emotionally unstable. If you are an emotional basket case, you will fold when times get tough. You must rely on your financial education and, just as importantly, on your ability to separate emotions from investing. Read *Your Money & Your Brain*, by Jason Zweig; to better understand what lies beneath the surface. You must learn to harness your emotions if you hope to be a wise and successful investor.

The day-to-day activity of the stock market is driven by speculation. It is important to understand this significant point. Speculation (educated guesses) can drive the markets for days, months, and even years. Eventually the stock market will reflect reality, which happens to be the true value of the investments you own. We just don't know when this will happen.

Here is some good news: It doesn't matter what happens to your investment account tomorrow or next week or even next month. The wise investor is concerned about market returns over decades.

So why do I want you to lose $100,000? In getting to that point, you will have changed your ways. You will have become a different person. You will have become the educated and wise investor.

The single greatest threat to your financial well-being is the hyperactive broker or advisor. The second greatest threat to your financial well-being is the false belief that you can trade on your own, online or otherwise, and attempt to beat the markets by engaging in stock picking or market timing. Finally, the third greatest threat to your financial well-being is paying attention too much of the financial media, which is often engaged in nothing more than "financial pornography." This conduct generates ad revenues for them and losses for investors who rely on the misinformation that is their daily grist.

- **Daniel Solin,** *The Smartest Investment Book You'll Ever Read*

Stock Market Returns

The numbers reflect the returns of the S&P 500 Index (large companies in the United States). The data was retrieved from the S&P 500 Dow Jones Indices. Reinvested yearly dividends are included. Losing years are highlighted. Focus on capturing as much of the market return as possible. Index funds do just that.

Year	S&P 500 Total Return
1992	7.62%
1993	10.08%
1994	1.32%
1995	37.58%
1996	22.96%
1997	33.36%
1998	28.58%
1999	21.04%
2000	-9.10%
2001	-11.89%
2002	-22.10%
2003	28.68%
2004	10.88%
2005	4.91%
2006	15.79%
2007	5.49%
2008	-37.00%
2009	26.46%
2010	15.06%
2011	2.11%
2012	16.00%

66

RUBBER BANDS CAN HURT

There are a few simple rules that will help you shrink the wide world of investing to a more manageable and understandable size. One of these rules can be understood by looking at how rubber bands work.

Please pick up a rubber band to help me make my point. This is going to be really tricky, so be ready. What happens when you pull on a rubber band? Yes, I mean what happens when you pull on it until it is stretched to the max, and then you let go? Does it pop back to where it started? Now I know what you are probably thinking: *well, duh, of course it pops back.* You now understand the investing concept of regression to the mean (also referred to as reversion to the mean).

Regression to the mean tells you that what goes up must come down. Whether you are dealing with stocks, bonds, gold, oil, or any other type of traded security, it will come back (prices will fall or rise) to its historical average at some point in the future (usually when you least expect it). Yes, there will be a few lonely voices that will tell you how things have gotten out of hand, but the crowd will drown them out as they tell you to get in before its too late!

This brings us to the idea of *recency bias.* Recency bias explains the phenomenon of letting what just happened in the investment world overly affect our investment decision-making. Let's say Gold has gone up 25 percent per year over the last three years. This causes us to think it will go up 25 percent again this year (plenty of Gold commercials will help you with this kind of thinking). That is unlikely. The historical mean on gold is around 4 percent. What goes up, must come down, which means you could see a pretty severe drop in the value of that investment.

Human beings are very good at noticing what has just happened, but we are not very good at looking back over long periods of time when making our financial decisions. This causes us to make decisions based on what has only recently occurred. This is a really bad idea, and it is important that you avoid making this mistake.

Do not chase the winners. A great deal of research has provided empirical data that shows us the fallacy of chasing winners while we attempt to avoid the losers. The five-star mutual fund (best performing investment) this year may be the one-star mutual fund (worst performing investment) next year. They are shooting stars, and that means they will flame out at some point in the future.

This brings us back to the rubber band. If you pulled that rubber band to its extreme nine times, and then let go only to hurt your finger when it snapped back all nine times, would you try it a tenth time? Or would you accept how rubber bands work and save yourself from more pain and suffering?

WARNING: Be skeptical of the bait-and-switch game some financial firms and salespeople will try to play on you. Here is how it works. They will roll out the latest investment that beat the current index, proving it can be done. Don't be fooled. They are calling the Super Bowl champion AFTER the game has been played! Predicting past performance is easy. Predicting future performance is not.

There is no way to choose the best managers in advance. I have calculated the results of employing strategies of buying the funds with the best recent-year performance, best recent two-year performance, best five-year and ten-year performance, and not one of these strategies produced above average returns. I calculated the returns from buying the best funds selected by Forbes magazine … and found that these funds subsequently produced below average returns.

- **Burton Malkiel**, *A Random Walk Down Wall Street*

Shooting Stars

The chart provides data taken from the mutual fund tracking agency, Morningstar. This illustration shows how the top 10 mutual funds performed since the year 2000. Going from number 1 to number 2,042 happens more times than you and I might imagine. The message should be clear, do not chase the stars!

Mutual Fund	2000	2001	2002	2003	2004
Evergreen Health Care	1	2,042	3,952	493	3,241
Manning % Napier Life	2	309	3,153	2,236	4,747
Munder Health	3	4,013	4,743	459	2,076
BlackRock Global	4	2,459	1,371	185	8
Allianz RCM Biotech	5	4,225	4,785	962	1,366
Eaton Vance World	6	2,810	4,219	2,503	3,549
Icon Energy	7	2,512	1,906	1,750	32
JennDry Jenn Health	8	2,333	4,605	810	154
Allianz RCM	9	3,544	4,267	2,319	1,995
Fidelity Select	10	4,116	2,178	2,351	22

67

CAN YOU BEAT A PRO?

I know there are some of you who think you are so savvy that you can outsmart the next guy when it comes to buying and selling individual stocks. I think you are mistaken. There is absolutely no reason for you to trade individual stocks as you attempt to make money based on your abilities to pick the winners and avoid the losers.

Let's face it, many of us like the challenge of outdoing others, whether it is in a game of basketball, a round of golf, or maybe beating the stock market. Many men can be especially bad at overestimating their skills in competitive events. That makes us human, but it also makes us vulnerable to people who will take advantage of this weakness.

It is estimated that 90 percent of the time you purchase or sell an individual stock, you are actually competing with professionals on Wall Street. These are men and women who spend their lives doing this. They even have computer programs that enhance their abilities using algorithms that play out scenarios before they actually happen! Trading with these people is the equivalent of you walking up to Tiger Woods, one of the best professional golfers in the world, and challenging him to a round of golf. You will lose, and it will not be pretty.

Buying individual stocks based on a broker's recommendation is ridiculous, and that's being kind. This also applies to exchange traded funds (ETFs) when they are traded as individual stocks, which happens way too often. Stop trying to outsmart your fellow human beings. You will fail more times than you will succeed.

ETFs, which are nothing more than packaged index funds, should only be used when investing for many years and preferably decades. Most people fail to do this, which is why I recommend you avoid ETFs (they also don't work well when dollar cost averaging your money into the market). Avoid trading any security based on short-term valuations and predictions. Do not speculate. Do not play a game you cannot win, it's that simple.

You are wasting your hard-earned money by paying commissions to a broker who is in no way qualified to guide you through that maze called Wall Street. Brokers (this includes your local financial advisor) are no smarter than you when it comes to selecting winning individual stocks. The system of individual stock picking is rigged against you and in favor of the financial industry. Don't play that loser's game.

Do I have some vendetta against brokers to include life insurance agents? Not really. Many individuals in the financial industry are just trying to make a buck in a system that was built long before they ever showed up to work there. Some are honest and some aren't.

Maybe I detest the big brokerage houses that feed off the average individual's financial ignorance. Actually, I do. They remind me of those dastardly ticks that you may find feeding off your poor helpless dog. Those blood-sucking parasites devour your dog's blood until they get so damned big, they explode. *Stay away from parasites.*

If there are 10,000 people looking at the stocks and trying to pick winners, 1 in 10,000 is going to score, by chance alone, a great coup, and that's all that's going on. It's a game, it's a chance operation, and people think they are doing something purposeful… but they're really not.

- **Merton Miller,** Winner of the 1997 Nobel Laureate in Economics

68

5.75 + 6.11 = 0?

I am sure most of you excelled in your math courses in school, but did you know that 5.75 + 6.11 = 0? Yes, in the world of investing, these numbers add up to zero, something that you will never see in those scholarly textbooks.

What do you say we take a look at how this equation works, and why you need to understand it when dealing with the financial "helpers" that saturate the financial industry.

When you go to a financial advisor and purchase a mutual fund, you are almost always going to pay a load (commission). Most of the time, when purchasing a mutual fund you will end up with class A shares, also called a front-end load. This is where the math starts to get confusing and illogical, at least for you, the investor.

Much of the time, class A shares will cost you 5.75 percent of your initial investment on a mutual fund trading stocks. Here is an example: You invest $1,000 in the hottest mutual fund of the year (bad idea), and as you give the broker your hard-earned money, he takes his cut (5.75 percent) leaving you with $942.50 to invest. I guess you have to make 5.75 percent to get back to $1,000, right? Sorry, that will only get you back to $996.69.

What will you have to earn to reach your initial investment of $1000? You guessed it: 6.11 percent. If you want to get back to where you started, which is $1,000, you will need to earn 6.11 percent after that initial 5.75 percent is siphoned off to the salesperson. 5.75 + 6.11 = 0.

Never pay a commission when investing your money.

Commissions come out of your pocket, and ultimately they reduce your return on investment. They put you in a hole, and you have to dig your way out. Here are a few basics on other types of loads: There are class B shares that charge you commissions when you sell (also called rear-end commissions, aptly named, if you ask me) and class C shares (which screw you with high costs the whole time you own the mutual fund).

Paying a commission to purchase a mutual fund is for the ill informed. There is no reason to do it once you understand your investment math. The smarter you become as an investor, the better the financial industry behaves. They have no choice but to change when YOU become a wise and efficient investor.

This means you avoid all financial salespeople and all of their commissions. You have become wise to the game they play, and you choose not to participate. Those so called experts lose their power over you once you understand how the game is played.

You can do the arithmetic. Why would you automatically accept a loss on your money? You do not have to be an accountant to see how these numbers don't add up in your favor. The math is a little nutty in the financial world. Understanding it will help you become the wise investor.

The investment business is a giant scam. Most people think they can find managers who can outperform, but most people are wrong. I will say that 85 to 90 percent of managers fail to match their benchmarks. Because managers have fees and incur transaction costs, you know that in the aggregate they are deleting value. You want to keep your fees low. That means avoiding the most hyped but expensive funds, in favor of low-cost index funds.

- **Jack Meyer,** former president of the Harvard Management Company

69

THE CASH COW

The annuity is a favorite of brokers and life insurance agents. Why do you think that is? Annuities are laden with commissions and high fees. It is the cash cow that keeps on producing. An annuity is an investment where you give a lump sum of money to an insurance company, and in return they promise a certain yield on the money you have invested.

Whether we are discussing the fixed, variable, or equity-index annuity, most investors should avoid these products at every turn. This will be easy if you follow some simple advice. *Avoid the milkmen who sell them.* The folks who end up with these poor investments are the ones who spend their days in the office of a broker or life insurance agent. These people are very good at selling. You don't need what they are peddling, and you certainly cannot afford it.

Insurance is big business in America and throughout the world. The insurance industry has been able to lobby politicians for all kinds of special considerations regarding what they can sell, and they love selling annuities.

Annuities involve a lot of projections (which tend to be inflated to entice you), a whole lot of fees (most annuities average over 2 percent in fees per year), and plenty of commissions (they can run up to 10 percent at the beginning and up to 7 percent if you attempt to leave early).

Annuities are sold to you as great investments for tax deferral and guaranteed returns over time. They benefit the salesperson and the insurance firm, not you (the insurance company pays the salespeople fat commissions and then lock up your money over long periods of time as they charge those outrageous yearly fees). Stay away!

If you let a broker or insurance agent educate you on these types of products, you will get sold. It's that simple. There may be one exception: The immediate-fixed annuity. This type of annuity requires a lump-sum initial payment, and in return the insurance company provides you a paycheck for the rest of your life. This should be done with great care, and that means doing plenty of research on the issue. I would recommend vanguard.com if you feel this option is right for you.

There are more reasons to hate annuities. They lack liquidity. It will be hard to get your money out without paying those hefty surrender penalties. Also, do not be swayed by the initial teaser rate. The agent will promise you a high introductory interest rate as a way to entice you. That rate is temporary and will soon drop, but only after your money is locked up and difficult to get out. Don't fall for that pitch. To learn more go here: http://www.youtube.com/watch?v=9-HSrtO5Dcw.

I hope I have clearly explained why you should avoid annuities and the salespeople who push them. As for the poor souls who currently own them, you do have options. You can move your annuity by doing a 1035 tax-free exchange into a commission-free and low-fee annuity at a place like Vanguard. This must be done with great care to avoid costly redemption commissions. Do your research BEFORE making this very delicate move.

Your financial advisor/broker/life insurance agent will not be happy with your decision to move your money, and that is a sign that you are moving in the right direction. Stay away from the cash cow!

Beware of brokers and insurance agents eager to escort your cash to another annuity. Investors get switched from one mediocre annuity to another all the time because brokers receive healthy commissions every time they convince someone to jump.

- **Daniel Solin,** *The Smartest Retirement Book You'll Ever Read*

70

DEATH INSURANCE

Death insurance (let's call it what it is) is a multibillion dollar industry. Some of the largest companies in the world are insurance companies. Why do you think that is? Please allow me to say something that the death insurance company will not tell you: Do not go to a death insurance agent and expect unbiased advice.

If you could make a much higher income (let's say a $3,000 commission) by selling one type of death insurance (cash-value policies such as whole life, universal life, or variable life) instead of another (term life with a commission of $300), which type of policy would you sell? Should we be surprised that most policies sold by death insurance agents are the cash-value policies?

Death insurance should be purchased to provide for the people who count on your income to survive. If no one relies on your income to live, it is very likely you do not need death insurance.

If you are concerned about burial costs, build your emergency savings or retirement accounts up to the amount you will need. Death insurance should not be purchased to bury loved ones. Now let's move on to the folks who do need death insurance.

Avoid all cash-value death insurance policies and the death insurance agents who sell them. Go online to one of the many term insurance clearinghouses (accuquote.com and term4sale.com are two examples) and purchase directly from them. They will look far and wide for the best policy at the lowest price.

Term life insurance is plain vanilla life insurance. It is cheap and affordable. Select an ART (annual renewable term) or a level term policy (five, ten, or twenty years, for example) that fits the time period you need. How much will you need? Figure on some amount roughly six to ten times your yearly income.

Make a plan on what to do with the insurance payout if that day comes and discuss it with your family. Providing for them is important, teaching them what to do with that money is just as important. Make sure there is a file that covers all of the information that will be needed if the day comes. Death insurance received upon a death is not taxed under the vast majority of circumstances. Plan accordingly.

The death insurance agent and his company conspire to sell you expensive, complicated products that benefit them. If you have a cash-value policy and you decide you need some amount of death insurance, I would consider getting rid of the cash-value policy AFTER you have purchased a term policy. Make sure you can pass a physical before making the move.

Still not sure? Go to thecrazymaninthepinkwig.com and hit on the insurance tab. There you can learn what other independent sources have to say on this very important subject.

How would I buy life insurance? I would start with low-cost term insurance, expecting to cancel it when I retire or when my kids are grown and my spouse is self-supporting. I'd find the insurer through a quote service. I'd build up investments somewhere else, in retirement funds, stock-owning mutual funds, Treasury securities and real estate, to guarantee my security. I would buy no life insurance on any of my children.

- **Jane Bryant Quinn,** *Making the Most of Your Money*

Whole Life vs. Term Life

Stated below are quotes received from a life insurance company selling a whole life policy and a term clearinghouse selling a ten-year-level term policy. Let's take a look at how much each policy will cost over different periods of time.

<u>Male: 25 years old, Non-smoking</u>

<u>$500,000 policy</u>

<u>Whole Life</u>		<u>Term</u>
$400	<u>Per month</u>	$14.16
$4,800	<u>1 year later</u>	$169.92
$48,000	<u>10 years later</u>	$1,699.20

The difference in cost:

$46,300.80

71

THAT IS A BIG YACHT!

I have one more story for you, and it should help wrap up our discussion of the investing business. I have heard it told in many ways by many different people. I am passing it on to you with my own small twist. It should help in putting together all that we have covered up to this point.

Once upon a time, there was an investment broker who sold life insurance, annuities, individual stocks, mutual funds, gold, silver, and even some commercial real estate. He was "licensed up" as they say in the financial business.

This financial "helper" was very successful, in that he made a large amount of money based on commissions and bonuses, and he had plenty of pretty stuff to show for it. Of course, this expert needed clients if he wanted his lifestyle to continue, and just as luck would have it, in walked his next *victim*.

The smooth-talking agent was dressed to the hilt in his sharp William Fioravanti business suit with a Golden Fleece Seven-Fold Micro Medallion Tie, and of course he was wearing his elegant Louis Vuitton dress shoes. Looking the part is very important in this business.

The new client was impressed with what he saw, and without batting an eye; the agent invited his prospective customer to take a trip down to the marina to see his beautiful new yacht. The potential client was ushered out of the office and seated in the agents lovely new Mercedes-Benz SL 65 AMG (R231). This car was spotless and exquisite in every way. The agent revved up the motor and sped out of his private parking lot, headed for the lovely marina.

After a short trip, the two arrived at the dock. The prospective client stepped out of the car and was amazed by what he saw. There was a gorgeous yacht only thirty feet away, and it belonged to the man who had just chauffeured him to this picturesque marina. The agent quickly invited his future client onto his very large and beautiful yacht. It was awesome!

As they reached the deck, the agent pointed to an even bigger yacht just across the bay. The yacht belonged to his boss. Then he pointed to another yacht just a little farther down the way, and this yacht was even bigger. That yacht belonged to his boss's boss. *One day*, the agent stated, *it could be mine. I just have to play my cards right.*

After a couple minutes of looking around, a weird look crossed the prospective client's face; it was as if he were confused or unsure about what he was seeing. The agent asked the client if something was wrong. The client turned to the agent and asked a very simple question:

Where are the yachts that belong to the clients?

A multibillion-dollar financial industry uses the average person to achieve THEIR dreams, not yours. They feed off your lack of financial knowledge as you run to them for help. That will cost you dearly. You must become financially literate, not because you want a big yacht, but because you cannot afford to pay for his!

You have to give great credit to hyperactive brokers and advisors. They have told a story that feeds into human psychology at a host of different levels. They have successfully marketed skills they don't have. They are able to keep Hyperactive Investors so confused and disoriented that these poor folks don't realize there is a much better alternative. And by doing so, they have made a whole lot of money.

- **Daniel Solin,** *The Smartest Investment Book You'll Ever Read*

High Cost vs. Low Cost

Below, you will see fifty years of compounding costs on a $10,000 lump-sum investment earning a 9.4 percent annual return (historical return based on an asset allocation equaling 80 percent stocks and 20 percent bonds and cash). Note: No other money was added to the account.

The load demonstrates a yearly cost of 3 percent, based on commissions paid to the salesperson and fees paid to the financial institution (this could include cash-value life insurance policies, annuities, and managed load mutual funds to name just a few).

The no-load demonstrates an industry average of fees paid to no-load mutual funds managed by people who spend their days buying and selling a lot (no commissions, just fees).

The index shows the fees you would pay in a portfolio of index funds. The numbers represent what you lose by investing with "smart people" versus index funds. The choice should be clear.

$10,000 in fifty years

Type	Cost	You lose it	You keep it
Load	3.0%	$689,323	$193,706
No-Load	1.5%	$468,836	$414,193
Index	.09%	$39,278	$843,751

72

THE KNOWLEDGEABLE
INVESTOR

Knowledgeable investors become wise investors as they apply what they know to serve their best interest. Let's recap what we have learned over the last few chapters:

- Select your asset allocation, and then rebalance every year or so. Selecting your bonds and cash allocation based on your age is one approach. One size does not fit all, though. The key is to identify what is right for you and then stick to it.

- Buy the cheapest no-load index mutual funds you can find. Keep it simple, go to vanguard.com and focus on the lowest possible costs as you diversify over large sectors of the US and international economies.

- Own at least one total stock market index fund and at least one short or intermediate term bond index fund. You can easily buy one target date retirement fund that does all of this for you, including the periodic rebalancing.

- Stay away from commission-based brokers and advisors. You don't need these milkmen, foxes, and yacht owners.

- As your portfolio grows, diversify your investments further with an international stock index fund, a small-cap stock index fund, a large-cap value index fund, and a REIT index fund. Once again, a target date retirement fund will suffice.

- Disregard people who tell you there are better ways to invest your hard earned money. Becoming one of the top 20 percent of investors in the world is good enough.

- Check your funds infrequently. Once a year is perfectly acceptable. Be an investor; not a speculator and that means ignoring most of what you hear and see coming from media sources.

- Laugh at the day-to-day hyperbole that you see on television. Human beings cannot predict the future, but they continue to try.

- Take your emotions out of your investing decisions. Love your spouse, not your money. Harness your emotions while acknowledging they do exist. Know thyself.

- If you need excitement, go climb a mountain. Don't try to find it in your investments. Investing should be boring.

- If you need someone to hold your hand, get a girlfriend, a boyfriend, a therapist, or maybe a dog. Tell the financial industry you have this covered.

- Stay the course. Buy and hold your investments, and just ignore the market-timing experts who are wrong more times than they are right. You are the knowledgeable investor.

Invest in low-turnover, passively managed index funds, and stay away from profit-driven investment management organizations. The mutual fund industry is a colossal failure resulting from its systematic exploitation of individual investors as funds extract enormous sums from investors in exchange for providing a shocking disservice. Excessive management fees take their toll, and manager profits dominate fiduciary responsibility.

- **David Swensen,** Chief Investment Officer of Yale University

73

THE TRANSFER

The day will come when you will need to transfer your money from one institution to another. Maybe you will transfer money out of your 401(k) from your old job. Maybe you have come to your senses and decided to move your investments away from your local broker and into those boring and very efficient index funds at Vanguard. To learn more, go here: https://investor.vanguard.com/what-we-offer/401k-rollovers/401k-403b-to-ira-rollover-benefits. This requires action by YOU.

You must be willing, able, and knowledgeable about what you are doing when you start moving money around. There is a great deal of money at stake, and I can promise you the financial industry knows this and will be there with their salespeople when that time comes.

The people at Vanguard will spend the needed time with you as you follow through on the process. They will make sure the paperwork is filled out correctly. They will answer your questions, and they do this at no cost. How do I know? I have done it, and I have helped hundreds of other people do it. You can do it. KEY POINT: They will not pick the funds for you. You must do the research and select the funds that are right for you (recommended funds were listed earlier in the book).

It is important that you put together a plan that reduces investment costs and taxes when you transfer your money. Many people have multiple retirement accounts doing little or nothing because they have been neglected. Find out exactly where those funds are, how you can access them, and when to start taking action to get YOUR money under YOUR control.

Here is a quick note on what not to do: Do not cash out your retirement account. That will end up costing you dearly (penalties and taxes). Focus on moving the money from one institution to another. It should not touch your hands.

Why should you do a transfer? It is in your best interest, that's why. Whether you are forced to take action (you quit, are fired, retire, etc.) or you have simply identified a better option, it benefits you to move your money to a place where you are in control of it. This is why you should transfer money to a place like Vanguard. Paying no commission is another pretty big deal. Let's take a look.

Let's say a financial advisor is going to "help" you transfer $100,000 from your current retirement account to a load managed mutual fund that will pay him a big fat commission. At a 5.75 percent commission, you would pay $5,750. That money goes to the salesperson, not the mutual fund. By avoiding the middleman, you can put the entire $100,000 into the no-load index mutual funds that fit your needs. *You keep the $5,750.* You also reduce your yearly fees with those very efficient and inexpensive index funds. Of course, you know that by now, right?

Take the time to understand what you are doing, and only transfer money when you understand why you are doing it, where it is going, and how much it will cost you. You will probably end up transferring funds many times in your life as you move from one job to another. Take control.

Deep down, I remain absolutely confident that the vast majority of American families will be well served by owning their equity holdings in an all –U.S. stock-market index portfolio and holding their bonds in an all-U.S. bond-market index portfolio. … The rationale for a 100-percent-index-fund portfolio remains as solid as a rock. It's all about common sense.

- **John Bogle**, *The Little Book of Common Sense Investing*

74

STAY THE COURSE

Periodically, when times get rocky, you will be tempted to turn back from your journey toward financial happine$$. I have three words for you. *Stay the course.* Fear has stopped many people from reaching their goals. Folks have approached the summit only to find that monster they call fear standing in the way of reaching their dreams.

Some people fear success. Some people fear failure. Some people just fear fear! It is important to identify fear when it rises up and tries to thwart our decision-making. Fear is and always will be our enemy. This is why we must *stay the course.*

How is it that some people stick it out through thick and thin, and others turn tail and run when times get tough? While we could certainly find more than one reason, it generally comes back to a lack of faith in one's plan and one's ability to stick to that plan. This is why we need a plan. It helps us to *stay the course.*

Work your plan. A plan is what keeps a person grounded when times get tough, and there will be tough times, that we know. A plan has short-term and long-term goals that keep a person focused as they proceed forward in life. They *stay the course.*

Goals help in dealing with one or more periods of crisis, which will surely come along (life continues to throw us curve balls we never saw coming) When things don't go exactly how they are supposed to go, the plan helps a person calm their nerves as they continue to *stay the course.*

When the economy or stock market falters, and it will at times, we must check our emotions at the door. Emotions sometimes lead to irrational decisions. We feel that we must do something, anything, to stop the pain. Emotions can cause us to veer away from our journey toward financial happine$$. Don't let this happen to you. Here is a bit of news that you will rarely hear from those psychic financial media pundits: Many times the best thing to do is nothing. Stick to your plan, and when in doubt, *stay the course.*

Financial literacy empowers us. By learning about money, we can better understand the long history of the financial markets throughout the world. We can always refer back to times during which similar events occurred to similar people. Markets repeat themselves over and over and over. The people who survived those times without losing their shirts, or their minds, had something in common: They pushed fear aside, stuck to their plan, checked their emotions at the door, and *stayed the course.*

You can do it!

Sometimes we all need to hear those simple words. You are capable of achieving great things, but it requires the ability to stand apart from the crowd. (Pink wig, anyone?) The crowd may push us to do something that is not smart. The crowd wants you to freak out as they are freaking out. The crowd is not your friend. You must learn to identify this folly and ignore the crowd. Believe in yourself, and *stay the course.*

Formulate and stamp indelibly on your mind a mental picture of yourself as succeeding. Hold this picture tenaciously. Never permit it to fade. Your mind will seek to develop the picture.... Do not build up obstacles in your imagination.

- **Norman Vincent Peale**

75

CREATING WEALTH

There is a path one can take to create wealth over time. Identify that path. Get on that path. Stay on that path. Maybe most importantly, don't let others push you off that path. Here is that path:

- Believe in yourself and take responsibility for your financial life. You are the answer. You must capture this mindset before proceeding forward.

- Track your expenses carefully, and complete a net-worth statement every year. Track the money coming in and going out of your life as you design a simple and systematic program that is easy to follow over long periods of time.

- Draw up a financial plan that lists your short- and long-term goals. This is the blueprint that drives your actions and keeps you on track when life gets bumpy, and it will get bumpy. Goals help you define your priorities.

- Work on your report card. (1) Increase your income potential. (2) Reduce your debt to appreciating assets only. (3) Increase your savings rate. (4) Increase your investment return after costs. (5) Live far below your means. Over long stretches of time, these five habits will dramatically change your degree of wealth (and personal fulfillment). Master these habits.

- If you have debt, put aside a small amount of money for emergencies. Anywhere around $1,000 should do fine.

- Sell anything that does not bring true value to your life. Rid yourself of stuff.

- Use the extra money to pay off every debt you have except your mortgage. If you want to fund your company retirement plan up to the matching amount during this time, go right ahead.

- Once your debt is gone, go back and build your emergency account up to at least three months of living expenses. Pay yourself first; do not buy a home until you have accomplished these first eight steps. Be patient. It's worth it.

- Put 20 percent of your gross income into your company retirement plan and Roth IRA. Divide up the 20 percent as you like and add more if you wish at the beginning of each pay period. Focus on no-load index mutual funds whenever possible.

- Stay out of debt. Buy only real estate, a business, and a college education using credit, and only do those things with great care and plenty of preparation. Pay cash for everything else.

- Save for big-ticket items. Save money for big stuff that is beyond your monthly income and avoid monthly payments. This includes cars and trucks.

- Stay the course. Wealth is created slowly. Be patient as your journey unfolds. Stay on the path and show others the path.

The gratification of wealth is not found in mere possession or in lavish expenditure, but in its wise application.
                                                                    - **Miguel de Cervantes**

Stage VI

TO GIVE IS TO LIVE

76

THE ART OF GIVING

Nothing feels better than giving unconditionally to others. Now I know that is a big statement, but I am here to tell you it is the truth, as I know it. I am sure there are a few of you thinking that there just might be things better than giving, but I stand by my statement. Let's take a closer look as I attempt to make this very important point.

First, let's discuss one myth about giving: Giving is when money exchanges hands from one party to another. There are many ways in which you can give; giving money is just one of them.

You can give of your time. You can give of your possessions. You can give of your experience. You can give of your expertise. You can even give an attitude. Do not discount how far a positive, optimistic attitude can go in helping others in their time of need. The point is, don't limit yourself to just giving money.

Open your mind toward giving as a way of living a compassionate, kind, and empathetic life. You change lives (including your own) when you focus your efforts on giving to others. This means giving to anyone and everyone along this journey that we call life. Embrace this mindset and your life will change forever.

Giving is one of the few things in life where all parties are guaranteed to benefit in the arrangement. When you give, you receive in ways that cannot be easily explained or written about. Many things in life are hard to describe. The feeling of giving is one of those things. *Learning to let go and give is done by the heart, not the head.*

Think back to the last time you truly gave of yourself to someone or some thing. How did you feel? I am betting it felt pretty darn good to help another human being or maybe a four-legged friend. Now here is the next question: How did it feel the last time you bought stuff? Don't just think about the moment of acquisition, but also think about how you felt days or weeks after the purchase.

Buying stuff provides a momentary rush of what feels like happiness, but it quickly fades. Giving provides that same feeling, but here is the kicker: It stays with you long after the moment of giving has occurred. That sustained feeling is what makes giving worth so much more. Giving will bring inner peace and joy into your life.

Now you may be asking what giving has to do with this money stuff. Here is one of those obvious points that I like to make: It is harder to give when you are broke. When you are stressed out about your debt and paying your bills, there is less of you to give.

Financial freedom empowers us to give in many different ways. It connects us with other living creatures on this planet. This is something that stuff cannot do and will never do. Becoming rich should not be the purpose of a financial literate life. Acquiring bigger and better stuff is not the purpose.

Reaching a high level of happiness is the ultimate reward for empowering others and ourselves with our newfound financial education. *What are your talents, and how can you help others?* Answer this question, and you will be well on your way toward a happy and meaningful life.

When I chased after money, I never had enough. When I got my life on purpose and focused on giving of myself and everything that arrived into my life, then I was prosperous.

- **Wayne Dyer**

The Fulfillment Curve: Reaching Higher

We have made it back to the fulfillment curve, but now we are ready to take it to the next level. That arrow that moves you beyond enough takes you to a much higher level of fulfillment.

Capture this message of giving, and you'll find your way toward inner peace and lasting happiness. To give is the way to live.

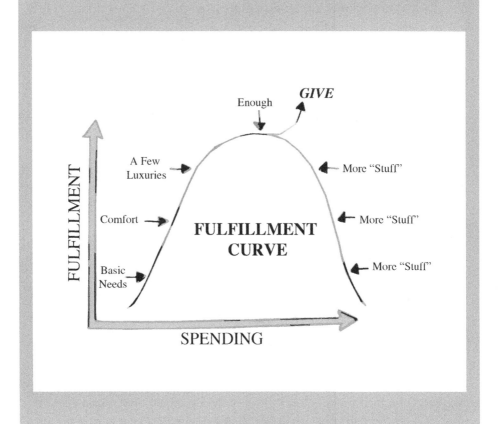

77

ONE, TWO, THREE

It is possible to live your financial life in three distinct phases: the collection phase, the preservation phase, and the giving phase. (There will be different degrees of overlap between each phase as transitions take place.) Let's take a moment to break each phase down as we clearly describe the importance each one can play in, not only your financial life, but also your life in general.

The *collection phase* is when you collect your wealth. This all starts with your belief in your abilities, followed by your financial education, and ultimately accomplished by your actions. The collection phase can last for many decades. Education starts you down this path. Action keeps you on this path.

Accumulating wealth takes time, courage, and plenty of patience as you live a life of ups and downs. Believe it or not, this can be the easiest of the three phases to master. What can be difficult is knowing when to transition to the next phase of your life. You will need to rely on your education and your instincts to tell you when it's time to make the big jump to the preservation phase.

The *preservation phase* is where you transition from collecting wealth and, instead, you manage your wealth wisely so as to preserve it over long periods of time. This is accomplished through your continued financial education and understanding of the concept of *enough*.

You start to dial back your time and energy on accumulating money (and stuff) and start to look at ways in which to share your money, your time, and your energy with the people and organizations you care about.

This phase can last for years and maybe decades, but gradually it must also come to an end as you transition into the final phase of your life. Why? There is nothing to be gained by being the richest man in the cemetery. Preserving your wealth should lead to something far beyond a big bank account. This brings us to the giving phase.

The *giving phase* is the final stage of your life. This is the time where you start distributing your money, your time, and your energy to the people and organizations that are dear to your heart. KEY POINT: Throughout your life, you will have the ability to give in many ways that do not involve money. I encourage you to find ways to give, even when you are in the previous two phases. Make giving a way of life, and this phase will come naturally to you when the time comes.

The giving phase can be a very challenging time as you try to identify how and where you are going to give. There is no perfect way to live out this phase. You must find YOUR way, and that will take some soul searching and maybe some starts and stops as you attempt to try things outside of your comfort zone. Let yourself go, and be open to creative ways to give. Don't worry about making mistakes. False starts are part of the journey. It's okay to start over. Many people do.

Notice there is no "all about me" phase. Spending your money on bigger homes, more expensive cars, and the latest-and-greatest clothing and technology will not bring happiness into your life. You can give to others what you have and what you know based on your desire to serve others. This may be the stage where you find YOU.

I don't know what your destiny will be, but one thing I know: the only ones among you who will be really happy are those who will have sought and found how to serve.

- **Albert Schweitzer**

78

THE FINANCIAL LITERACY JOURNEY

Yes, this is a repeat lesson. What have you learned? Will this lesson speak to you differently than the first time you read it? I hope so. It's time to be financially free. It's time to be happy.

- *I am.* I am the answer to my financial future. I can make it a total mess, or I can make it a glorious masterpiece. All of this hinges on me. I am the answer.

- *Knowledge.* I must educate myself before making financial decisions. This will involve a commitment to education outside the classroom with teachers, not salespeople.

- *ACTION.* I must take action with what I learn. Being financially smart and doing nothing with the information will accomplish nothing. I must get it done!

- *Keep Doing.* I must keep doing what is right financially one week, one month, one year, and one decade at a time. I will stay persistent as I develop the right habits (pay myself first automatically at the beginning of the month) that I perform time and time again.

- *Just say NO!* I will say no to materialism (defining myself by the stuff I own) and the crocodiles (salespeople who feed off my financial ignorance). This will free up money to be saved, invested, and given away.

- *Patience.* Time is on my side. Be patient as my financial plan unfolds over long periods of time. Get rich slowly through compound interest. My money will make me money.

- *Financial Freedom.* Financial freedom can be achieved if I am willing to truly commit myself totally to the process of following through on my financial plan. Saving = Freedom = Opportunities.

- *Live MY Dreams.* Live the life of my dreams and not someone else's. Financial freedom provides me the opportunity to do just that. Find my path, and live it!

- *Give.* Live to give. Learning to be grateful for what I have and identify ways to give unconditionally, will set me free. Giving to the people and organizations I believe in will bring meaning and inner peace to my life.

- *Happiness.* Happiness comes to those who follow their dreams and share what they know and have with others. I want to be happy. I will be happy. The answers to life are with me. Find ME, and I will find my path to happiness.

I have provided you with many of the tools that will help you maneuver successfully down your financial literacy journey. It is now up to you and what you do with that knowledge. It's time to ACT.

Be the change you wish to see in the world. - **Gandhi**

79

YOUR JOURNEY

80

THE BEGINNING

Your journey has been left blank for a reason. Sometimes it's best to wipe our slate clean and start over. That is what I did once upon a time. This may be your time. I challenge you to read this book again, except I would like you to read it from back to front. A different perspective will draw different results.

I have one final story to share with you. This story explains the value of this message I am sharing and how it can help us and the people we love. I share it with a heavy heart and maybe a tear or two.

Once upon a time, there was a young man who came home for the holidays. He showed up with something other than presents. He came with knowledge, financial knowledge to be precise. As his father was sitting down with his favorite beverage, this young man sat beside him and started to share what he had learned. His father wasn't so sure, but he continued to listen to his very excited son.

The young man started to talk about this new world of money and how it had changed his life. He explained how it had empowered him and how he had been exposed to something new that he didn't know existed. His father continued to listen, but he still needed some convincing.

What could a young man without a college education teach this older man who had lived a long and rather difficult life? *Plenty* was the response from his enthusiastic and highly animated son. And at that, the young man showed his father the portfolio of assets he had accumulated. His father came to realize that his son had more money than he did. Maybe it was time to listen.

As you probably realize by now, I was that young man. Why do I tell this story? Financial literacy gave me the ability to help not only myself but also my father. We moved his life savings away from a broker who was churning his account (buying and selling securities often to increase the amount of commissions paid to the broker) and into a no-load index mutual fund that would not.

If you remember, at the beginning of this book, my father gave me *the boot* that I needed. I had finally found the opportunity to pay him back. We had come full circle, and that meant a great deal to me and I hope to him. There is little to nothing that means more in life than helping the people you love. I think deep down we all know that.

I owe a great deal to the teachers who have entered my life. They taught me that this money stuff is not as difficult as I thought, and I could not only learn about it, but I could help others learn about it too. What I did not realize at the time was how it would change my life beyond the spreadsheets and the investment accounts.

Financial literacy provided me a path to finding real and long-lasting happiness. I found inner peace and personal fulfillment as my journey played out over many years and multiple decades. *I found myself along that journey.* It can do the same for you if you're willing to challenge the world in which you live. YOU are the answer to how your life ultimately turns out.

Shape your environment or allow the environment to shape you. The choice is yours. The choice is always yours.

- **The "Crazy" Man in the Pink Wig**

Financial Happine$$ Day

April 30

Join me on April 30 of this year and for many years to come in celebrating Financial Happine$$ Day on planet earth. Wherever you are, I challenge you to wear that pink wig proudly. Whether you wear the pink wig on your jeans, your shirt, your shorts, or even your head, show the world where you stand as you communicate a very clear message:

I am the answer to my financial life!

The Contest

The "crazy" man in the pink wig intends to show you just how crazy he really is. In the year 2015, there will be a financial literacy contest to find out who the most financially literate people in the world are. I will be giving away money at this contest. How much?

$100,000!

It is now time to put my money where my mouth is. I will dig into my wallet (and I have a big wallet) and pull out $100,000. Five financially literate people will win $20,000. It could be YOU! You can go to thecrazymaninthepinkwig.com and hit on the contest tab to learn more details about this event as it approaches.

Every question on the test will come from this book or from my website. Review each chapter carefully and be able to explain it to a friend. This will demonstrate just how well you understand the material. Educating yourself and then sharing that knowledge will reinforce what you have learned on the different topics. It will also provide you the chance to help others with what you have learned.

Go to my website and study the attachments in detail. Watch my videos until you have them memorized. Study your tail off, and prepare to blow away the competition. Entering this contest will cost you $1. Can you afford it? I think you can. Get a study plan put together, stick to it, and make it happen.

Anyone can win this contest. You don't need a finance degree. You don't need a college degree. Hell, you don't even need a high school diploma! What do you need? You simply need the commitment to educating yourself beyond where you are at this moment in time. It is time to reach for financial happine$$!

Appendix A

Recommended Reading:
Selections from my teachers

Vicki Robin and Joe Dominguez

Your Money or Your Life (This book will change your life if you are open to its message. It is one of my favorites.)

Eric Tyson

Personal Finance for Dummies (I would start here if I was a beginner.)

Let's Get Real About Money (This book takes you to that next level financially and psychologically.)

Jane Bryant Quinn

Making the Most of Your Money (A book that covers everything you would like to know about money. This is a wonderful reference book.)

Smart and Simple Financial Strategies for Busy People (Jane helps busy people by telling them specifically what to do right now.)

Jonathan Clements

The Little Book of Main Street Money (A book written for the average person, it is easy to read and easy to understand.)

Burton Malkiel

A Random Walk Down Wall Street (A classic that provides insight into a world that can be mysterious to us all.)

John Bogle

The Little Book of Common Sense Investing (This is a great starter book on investing. You can trust John Bogle. I do.)

Common Sense on Mutual Funds (This book will teach you all you need and want to know about investing in mutual funds.)

William Bernstein

The Four Pillars of Investing (The finest book on investing I have ever read. This book will show you the past, the present and maybe the future.)

The Investors Manifesto (A great follow-up book. You might find this an easier read than his other books.)

Charles Ellis

Winning the Loser's Game (Investing becomes easier once we become informed about the business of investing and how we can conquer it.)

Jason Zweig

Your Money & Your Brain (Explains how our brains and our emotions work when it comes to money. It may blow your mind!)

Thomas Stanley

The Millionaire Next Door (A wonderful book that helps us see who the real millionaires are. It just may surprise you.)

The Millionaire Mind (Thinking like a millionaire comes before becoming a millionaire.)

Stop Acting Rich (You can be rich, or you can act rich. This book defines what habits place you in each group.)

Andrew Hallam

Millionaire Teacher: The Nine Rules of Wealth You Should Have learned in School (The average guy can do it.)

Dave Ramsey

The Total Money Makeover (Debt is your enemy. Kick it out of your life, or let it control your life. Dave will help you take control of your debt.)

Michael Mihalik

Debt is Slavery and 9 Other Things I Wish My Dad Had Taught Me about Money (This book is short, sweet, and to the point.)

Tim Kasser

The High Price of Materialism (You cannot afford it.)

Trent Hamm

The Simple Dollar (A regular guy changed his financial life. He demonstrates how he did it and how you can do it.)

Keith Cameron Smith

The Top 10 Distinctions between Millionaires and the Middle Class (Your thinking and your habits will define who you ultimately become.)

Daniel Solin

The Smartest Investment Book You'll Ever Read (This book is short and to the point. He tells you what to do and why.)

The Smartest Retirement Book You'll Ever Read (Mr. Solin is consistent in his approach. He tells you how to prepare for retirement and why.)

Sources

Chapter 3

1. Dominguez, J. R., & Robin, V. (1992). Your money or your life: Transforming your relationship with money and achieving financial independence. New York: Viking

Chapter 4

2. Greig's Blog, "Have you ever been told how they train a circus elephant?" Retrieved March 17, 2013, from http://www.px2.co.za/how-they-train-circus-elephants/

Chapter 17

3. Maxwell, J. C. (2008). Developing the leader within you: Developing the leaders around you. Nashville, Tenn: T. Nelson.

Chapter 19

4. Goldstein, R. (January 23, 2011). nytimes.com. In Jack LaLanne, Founder of Modern Fitness Movement, Dies at 96. Retrieved November 10, 2012, from http://www.nytimes.com/2011/01/24/sports/24lalanne.html? r=0.

Chapter 62

5. Dash, M. (April 24, 2000). businessweek.com. In When the Tulip Bubble Burst. Retrieved February 2, 2012, from http://www.businessweek.com/2000/00_17/b36780 84.htm.

Acknowledgments

Many people have helped me complete this book. I needed their guidance, their editing abilities, and maybe most of all, I needed their support. They came through with flying colors! I am very grateful to the people who helped make this happen. There are simply too many names to put down on paper, but you know who you are. Thank you from the bottom of my heart.

A book is not written in a few weeks or even in a few months (at least not by me). A book is written using a lifetime of experience and knowledge. When I think back to my family, friends, coaches, and teachers (in and outside the classroom), I am struck by how many wonderful people have entered my life and provided me insight when I needed it most. I needed assistance, and many of you were there to provide your help and support when I needed it most. Thank you for your help and that occasional kick in the butt that I needed.

I also want to thank people I have never met. Those authors who write books that change our lives are saviors to many of us. They expand our world far beyond anything we could have imagined. They show us what we can become and where we can go. They enlighten us and maybe most importantly, they provide hope as we try to figure out where we fit in this crazy world. Thank you for taking the time and making the effort to teach a young kid from a small town in Iowa. You changed my life, and I truly appreciate what you have done to make this world a better place.

At times our own light goes out and is rekindled by a spark from another person. Each of us has cause to think with deep gratitude of those who have lighted the flame within us.

- **Albert Schweitzer**

Illustrations

The illustrations in the book, including the book cover, were designed and created by some very talented ladies.

Book cover creator: Meghan Kelley
Book cover design: Faith Wittrock
Stage V illustration: Melanie Walde
All other illustrations: Faith Wittrock

Glossary

1035 exchange: A transfer of money from one insurance policy (this includes annuities) to another. This type of exchange can be used when moving money out of high-fee insurance policies and into low-fee insurance policies. Educate yourself carefully regarding any possible surrender charges.

401(k): A defined contribution plan offered by a corporation to its employees to set aside tax-deferred income for retirement purposes. This is the place where you can grow your money tax deferred (traditional version) or tax-free (Roth version).

403(b): A retirement plan offered by nonprofit organizations, such as universities and charitable organizations, rather than corporations. This is simply a company retirement plan that goes by a different name. Fees tend to be high compared to other defined contribution plans.

457(b): A retirement plan offered by some nonprofits, as well as state and local governments. This is another company retirement plan that goes by a different name. One big plus with this type of plan is the elimination of the 10% penalty for early withdrawal.

529 Plan: An education savings plan designed to help parents save for their children's college education. Go straight to the state and bypass the broker. Shop around. Some states have poor choices and others provide very good options that include index funds from Vanguard.

Active management: The attempt to uncover securities (stocks and bonds, for example) that the market has misidentified as being under or overvalued. This involves outsmarting and outmaneuvering the other smart people in the room. The past has shown us it doesn't work with any degree of consistency (pure chance basically). Avoid the people who tell you they can provide it. They can't.

Annual renewable term (ART): Term life insurance that provides coverage for one year and is automatically renewed based on the needs of the person who purchases the policy.

Annuity: An investment that is a contract backed by an insurance company. Its main benefit is that it allows your money to compound and grow without taxation until withdrawal. The main drawbacks include high commissions, high fees, and difficulty in extracting your money. The financial industry loves annuities. That is a good reason to question the benefit of an annuity to you. Stay away, far away.

Asset allocation: The process of dividing up one's securities among broad asset classes (stocks, bonds, and real estate, for example). This may include domestic and foreign stocks and bonds. The asset allocation should be identified only after the investor identifies their risk tolerance, time horizon, and specific goals that are unique to their particular situation.

Asset class: A group of assets with similar risk and expected return characteristics. Cash, debt instruments (think bonds), real estate (REITS or rental real estate), and equities (stocks) are a few examples. There are more specific classes that are broken down within an asset class, such as large and small company stocks and domestic and international stocks.

Bear market: A period when the stock market experiences a strong downward swing. It is often accompanied by an economic recession. During a bear market, the value of stocks can decrease significantly (20 percent is the barometer used by most). This is when most "experts" tell you to get out the market. This is also the time when the asset is on sale.

Benchmark: A standard against which mutual funds and other investment vehicles can be judged. Small-cap managers should be judged against a small-cap index such as the Russell 2000 Index. Large-cap growth funds should be judged against a large-cap growth index such as the S&P 500 Index. Comparing apples to apples is the point of using the proper benchmark.

Bond: A loan investors make to a corporation or government. The investor provides the capital, and the other party promises a specified return. Bonds generally pay a set amount of interest on a regular basis. All bonds have a maturity date when the bond issuer must pay back the bond at full value to the bondholders (the lenders).

Broker: A person who acts as an intermediary for the purchase or sale of investments. Almost all brokers are paid on commission, which creates a conflict of interest with their clients (also known as victims). The more the broker sells the more money he makes. This is called churning, and it is illegal but difficult to prove in a court of law. Stay away from them.

Capital gain: The profit from selling your stock at a higher price than the price for which it was purchased. Example: You bought a mutual fund at $60 per share, and you sell it five years later for $90 per share. Your profit is $30 per share. If your investment is outside of a retirement account, you will pay a capital gains tax on that profit. This will not apply (in the year in which you sold the asset) to an investment that is in a retirement plan.

Cash-value life insurance: This is the type of life insurance that most life insurance agents recommend. In a cash-value policy, you buy life insurance coverage but also get a savings account to boot. The investment returns tend to be poor because of the high commissions and high fees that come out in the early years of the policy. Stay way.

Churning: When a broker has you buying and selling your investments often to feed HIS bank account. A broker needs a lot of activity on your account; otherwise the commissions will not be enough to feed his lifestyle. Avoid brokers, and you will avoid being churned. It doesn't get any simpler than that.

Consumer debt: Debt on consumer items that depreciate in value over time. Car loans, furniture loans, and credit card balances are some examples. This type of debt will reduce your wealth while enriching the businesses and salespeople who market this type of approach to buying.

Credit: A tax credit reduces your taxes dollar for dollar. Example: If you owe $8,000 in taxes and you have a $1,000 tax credit, your taxes owed will be reduced to $7,000. This is as close to a free lunch as Uncle Sam offers.

Debit card: This device has replaced the check. When you use a debit card, the cost of the purchase is deducted from your bank account.

Deductible: The deductible is the amount you pay when you file an insurance claim. Example: You have a car accident, and it was your fault. The damage to your vehicle and to others will be $5,000. If your deductible is $500, you will pay that amount and your insurance company will pay $4,500. High deductibles reduce your yearly premiums. Low deductibles raise your yearly premiums.

Deduction: An expense you subtract from your income to lower your taxable income. This may include: retirement accounts, interest and property taxes on a mortgage, charitable contributions, and moving expenses. A deduction is nice, but buying something just for the deduction is generally a bad idea. Getting thirty cents back for every dollar you spend will not help your bottom line.

Defined benefit plan: A pension that your employer promises you based on time with the company, your earnings, and usually your age. These are going away and being replaced with defined contribution plans. These types of plans are still widely available for state and federal employees. If you have one, count your blessings.

Defined contribution plan: A retirement plan funded primarily by the employee. It may come in the form of a traditional or a Roth version. Names of these types of plans are as follows: 401(k), 403(b), 457(b), and TSP (thrift savings plan). You must feed these accounts monthly and yearly if you want a comfortable retirement.

Diversification: Dividing investment funds among a variety of investments with different risk/return characteristics to minimize portfolio risk. A mutual fund that owns 3,000 companies is one example of diversification.

Dividend: The income paid to investors holding an investment. The dividend is a portion of a company's profits paid to its shareholders. For assets held outside retirement accounts, dividends are taxable in most cases.

Dollar-cost averaging: A fixed amount of money is invested regularly and periodically. When the price of the asset is down, more shares are purchased. When the price of the asset is up, fewer shares are purchased.

Effective tax rate: An individual's effective tax rate is calculated by dividing total tax expense by taxable income. This is the rate you actually pay in relation to your gross income.

Equity: Equity is a term often used to describe stocks. In real estate, it is used to describe the difference between how much your home is worth and how much you owe. Example: Your home is worth $200,000 and you owe $120,000. Your equity is $80,000.

Event risk: The risk that something unexpected will occur (war, political crisis, flood, tornado, hurricane, fire, etc.) that negatively impacts the value of a specific security. This is why we don't put our money in the sock drawer or stuff it in the mattress.

Exchange traded funds (ETFs): Like mutual funds, they can be created to represent virtually any index or asset class. Like stocks (but unlike mutual funds), they trade on a stock exchange throughout the day. They work for long-term, lump sum investing. They don't work for investors who trade often and/or dollar-cost average money into their investments.

Expense ratio: The operating expenses of a mutual fund expressed as a percentage of total assets. They cover manager fees, administrative costs, and sometimes marketing costs.

Fee-based financial advisor/planner: This term is used to describe how a licensed salesperson earns his or her money. Fee-based usually means the salesperson works on commissions from the investments he or she sells and some other method such as a percentage of money under management or an hourly fee. Avoid fee-based salespeople.

Fee-only financial advisor/planner: This term describes how a professional earns his or her money. The drawback with this type of planner is they generally require a large amount of money under management before they work with you.

FICO score: The score that most lenders use to identify an applicant's credit risk. The higher the score, the lower the interest rate and the more likely credit will be provided.

Fiduciary: The expert sitting across from you has an obligation to act in your best interest instead of his. When seeking financial advice, this is the kind of person you should seek. Sadly, they are hard to find.

Fixed annuity: An insurance contract in which fixed dollar payments are paid for the term of the contract. The insurance company guarantees both earnings and principal. A high initial teaser rate is generally offered to pull you in. High commissions and high fees make this a poor choice.

Fixed-interest mortgage: You lock in an interest rate on a specific period of time (usually fifteen or thirty years). The monthly payment will not change throughout the lifetime of the loan. The insurance and property taxes that are generally tied up with the loan will change over the years.

Hedonic treadmill: When you make more money or get more "stuff," your expectations and desires go up in tandem. You adapt. You continue to believe getting that next raise or that next big "thing" will be the answer to achieving happiness. You are never satisfied with what you have.

Home-equity loan: Also known as a second mortgage. With this type of loan, you borrow against the equity in your home. Using these types of loans can put your mortgage at risk. Tread lightly. I would avoid them.

Immediate fixed annuity: A life insurance contract that takes a lump sum provided by you and turns it into a pension for life. Your life expectancy, age, and gender are used to figure out the monthly payment you will receive. If you live longer than expected, you win. If you live fewer years than expected, they win.

Index mutual fund: A mutual fund designed to mimic the returns of a given stock market index. Examples would include: the S&P 500, the Wilshire 5000, and the Russell 3000. These types of funds are ultra-cheap, and because of the cost difference, they have consistently beaten managed mutual funds over short and long periods of time. Never pay a commission when selecting this option.

Individual retirement account (IRA): A retirement account that you open outside of your place of employment. There are many types: Roth (after tax) and traditional (before tax) are two. Which one you select will vary based on your current and projected tax situation. There are many rules as well as contribution limits to these accounts.

Institutional investors: Large investment organizations, including insurance companies, depositary institutions, pension funds, and philanthropies. Indirectly, your money is invested through them when you have a pension, give to a charity, etc.

International stock market mutual fund: Pooled stocks within a mutual fund that are invested in stock markets outside of the United States.

Investment Management Company: A company whose main business is holding securities of other companies for purely investment purposes. The investment company invests money on behalf of its shareholders, who in turn share in the profits and losses.

Junk bond: A bond rated below investment grade. These types of bonds are also called high-yield bonds. Many people own junk bonds as they chase yield (interest on your investment). You do not need junk.

Keogh plan: A tax-deductible retirement plan that is available to self-employed individuals. They are relatively easy to set up at your favorite investment management company, such as Vanguard.

Large-cap: Large-cap stocks are those companies considered big relative to other companies, as measured by their market capitalization. Large can be subjective.

Level term life insurance: Term life insurance that provides a fixed amount of coverage based on a fixed price over a fixed period of time such as five, ten, or twenty years.

Load mutual fund: A mutual fund sold with a sales charge and paid to the salesperson that initiates the action between the investor and the investment company. A load and a commission are one in the same.

Marginal tax rate: The rate of income tax (federal, state, and city if it applies) you pay on the last dollars you earn.

Mortgage life insurance: Mortgage life insurance pays off your mortgage if you die. This is sold during the mortgage buying process, as the lender tries to reduce their risk and increase their profit. It's expensive. Stay away.

Mutual fund: A portfolio of stocks, bonds, or other assets managed by an investment company. They provide wide diversification that is necessary and prudent for the average investor.

No-load mutual fund: A mutual fund sold without a sales or distribution fee. There is no commission attached to your investment.

Nominal return: Returns that have not been adjusted for inflation. These are the types of returns you will almost always see when reading a newspaper, a magazine, or listening to a presentation on investing.

Passive management: A buy-and-hold investment strategy. The passive management approach includes lower portfolio turnover, lower operating expenses and transactions costs, greater tax efficiency, consistent exposure to risk factors over time, and a long-term perspective.

Pension: A benefit offered by some employers. These plans (also known as defined benefit plans) generally pay you a monthly retirement income based on your years of service and former pay with the employer.

Real estate investment trust (REIT): A mutual fund that owns stock in shopping centers, apartment buildings, and other commercial real estate.

Real return: The nominal return minus the inflation rate. Example: You earn 5 percent on an investment and the inflation rate is running at 3.2 percent. Your real return would be 1.8 percent.

Rebalancing: The process of buying and selling portfolio components so as to maintain a target asset allocation.

Recency bias: An investor is overly influenced by recent events when selecting a particular asset.

Roth: A retirement plan that places your money into your selected investment accounts after the money has been taxed.

Russell 1000 index: This index is intended to track 1,000 of the largest publicly traded companies in America. It is used as a benchmark for large-capitalization stocks.

Russell 2000 index: This index is intended to track 2,000 of the smallest publicly traded companies in America. This index is used as a benchmark of small-capitalization stocks.

Russell 3000 index: This index tracks the Russell 1000 and 2000 index of companies. It is used to replicate the entire market of large and small companies.

Simplified employee pension individual retirement account (SEP-IRA): A retirement plan for self-employed people.

Standard & Poor's 500 Index: An index that measures the performance of 500 large-company US stocks.

Stock: Shares of ownership in a publicly held company. You can invest in stock by purchasing individual shares or by owning a stock mutual fund.

Survivorship bias: Mutual funds that die don't count against the overall return as if they never existed. Managed mutual fund historical returns would look much worse if all of the headstones were counted.

Target date retirement fund: This type of fund allocates your investments within the fund based on the date you select. A 2050 fund will be more aggressive (more stocks) than a 2030 fund (more bonds and cash).

Term life insurance: Cheap life insurance that has no cash value. It should be purchased when someone relies on your income to live.

Thrift Savings Plan (TSP): A defined contribution plan offered by the federal government to its employees (military and civilian).

Timeshare: You are renting a really nice place for a week or so during the year. They call it buying. Avoid them and the salespeople who push them. They are expensive to maintain and difficult to sell. Don't fall for the pitch.

Turnover: The portion of a portfolio that is traded in a given period of time. For example, a portfolio with an annual turnover of 300 percent will increase the costs by approximately 3 percent per year.

Universal life insurance: Cash-value life insurance that grew out of whole life insurance. Part investment and part insurance is the idea. Stay away.

Variable annuity: A life insurance contract providing future payments to the holder. The size of the future payments will depend on the performance of the portfolio's securities, as well as the investor's age at the time of annuitization and prevailing interest rates. Stay away.

Variable life insurance: A cash-value policy that has part of the account invested in investments like stocks and bonds that will fluctuate over time. Stay away. The costs are high and the returns are low.

Whole life insurance: Cash-value life insurance that provides level premiums over time. High commissions and high fees make this a bad deal.

Wilshire 5000 total market index: This index mimics the entire US stock market, which includes small, mid, and large capitalization companies. Use this index when identifying a total stock market fund to invest in.

The Fix

There is a fix to this problem of financial illiteracy in our modern world. Replace the commission-based salespeople with financial educators/counselors that get paid by the hour or project. Is this wishful thinking? No. It just takes the right kind of person or organization that is truly dedicated to serving the people under their care. Let's take a look at how this could become reality.

The financial educator/counselor will spend a great deal of time educating themselves about the world of money so they can pass that wisdom on to their clients. The more they know, the more they can help others. They eliminate any conflict of interest by eliminating commissions. They are not beholden to anyone except their clients. There are many fee-only financial planners that are serving their clients in a similar way right now. The problem is fee-only financial planners generally don't take on clients with less than $250,000. (For a fee-only financial planner in your area, go here: http://www.napfa.org.) We need someone who is going to help the average person. That could be YOU.

Will this kind of person or organization make as much money as the commission based operation? I seriously doubt it. There are more important things in this world than making more money. The financial educators can go to bed at night knowing they are truly helping others along their journey toward finding financial happine$$.

So how does this happen? One person and one financial organization at a time, that's how. We stop focusing on making more and more money and instead, focus on providing the highest level of financial guidance while making a modest amount of money. When you provide a quality product, word will spread. Here is one more thought I would like to leave with you. A reporter asked **Mahatma Gandhi**, "What is your message?" He said something that applies to us all.

My life is my message.

The Difference Makers

The people and organizations listed below are making a difference in the world. They are truly serving their communities in ways that go far beyond what can be explained in a book or on a spreadsheet. I would recommend using these sources to further your education on financial matters. Better yet, JOIN THEM!

Websites/Blogs

http://www.farnoosh.tv

http://www.mrmoneymustache.com

http://janebryantquinn.com

http://www.jonathanclements.com

http://www.bogleheads.org

http://askthemoneycoach.com

http://www.thesimpledollar.com

http://thefrugalmodel.com

https://www.facebook.com/UniFinancialLiteracyClub

http://andthenwesaved.com

http://www.getrichslowly.org

Something Extra

Use the addresses below to contact me. I always enjoy hearing from folks who are travelling somewhere along their financial literacy journey. I will provide help and support, but please do not ask for money. My money will be going to the contest.

I am available on a limited basis for speaking engagements. Contact me for information regarding dates and times. I am happy to share the message when others are ready to receive it.

You can give.

The contest is my approach in dealing with the financial illiteracy crisis in America today. This is why I am putting up my own money to make this happen. If you would like to give to this contest, you may send your contributions to the address shown below.

I am not asking you for money. I am simply providing you the opportunity to be part of something that is much bigger than you and me. Any monetary amount you select is fine, whether that is $1 or $1,000. Every dollar will go toward the contest (and future contests).

You have my word that your money will be used wisely and not syphoned off to pay for some lavish lifestyle. I am asking you to trust me. Follow your heart.

You may contact me directly to purchase a signed book or tee shirt. You can also go to my website to purchase the book (written, e-book, or audio) and/or the Financial University tee shirt. Prices are reflected on the next page.

Address: Mike Finley, 5402 Meadowlark Lane, Cedar Falls, Iowa 50613
E-mail: mikefinley@thecrazymaninthepinkwig.com
Website: Thecrazymaninthepinkwig.com

The cost per item includes shipping and handling. All Iowa residents please add 7 percent on top of your cost to cover the sales tax. The numbers are reflected below.

Cost of the book signed by the author: $25.00 (Iowans pay $26.75)

Cost of the t-shirt: $18.00, select a size when ordering (Iowans pay $19.26)

Cost of the book and t-shirt combined: $40.00 (Iowans pay $42.80)

If you would prefer to buy these items with your credit or debit card, please provide the following information through the contact page on my website or in an e-mail to the address you see on the previous page. You can also mail a letter through the US postal system. Your personal information will be guarded at all times. None of your information will be shared with other people or organizations. Please provide the following information in the format shown below.

Full Name: Please keep it as legible as possible

Card Type: Visa or MasterCard only

Credit or Debit: Identify how the card is being used

Credit Card Account Number: Entire number

Expiration Date of the Card: Month and year

Card Security Code: The three-digit code on the back of the card

Return Address: Where you want your purchase sent

E-mail Address: I will let you know when the product ships

Thousands of candles can be lighted from a single candle, and the life of the candle will not be shortened. Happiness never decreases by being shared.

- **The Buddha**

Made in the USA
Monee, IL
13 April 2021